for Marilyn —
who loves poetry
understands struggle
to find yourself,
your voice,
your heart!

Wildflowers in the Snow

10-23-04

Carolyn Wing Greenlee

Wildflowers in the Snow

First Printing
April 16, 2000

Editor: Daniel Worley
Layout and Design: Daniel Worley
Cover Design: Stephanie C. Del Bosco

Library of Congress Cataloging–in–Publication Data
Greenlee, Carolyn Wing, 1947–
    Wildflowers in the Snow / Carolyn Wing Greenlee.
        p. cm.
    ISBN 1-887400-26-5 (pbk.)
        1. Chinese American families—Poetry.
        2. Chinese Americans—Poetry. I. Title.

PS3557.R3959 W55 2000
813'.54—dc21

                                                    99-462157

Earthen Vessel Productions, 3620 Greenwood Dr., Kelseyville, CA 95451, USA
Printed in the United States of America   ISBN 1-887400-26-5

Wildflowers in the Snow

Earthen Vessel Productions

Foreword

Poetry and writing are, in my opinion, the most intimate of arts. I don't mean that heart and soul cannot be captured in other arts, but there is in poetry and writing a unique attribute: Whatever is captured is bound by "literal" tools. The writer's pallet—words, grammar, language—is always literal. By definition, writing desires and requires the communication of content. So I believe.

That accepted, it is my opinion that the work of any good poet exists, almost fossil-like, as the record of their path to the present. The Hungarian Moholy-Nage (1895-1946) contended that every object is a record of forces, over time, which have shaped and determined its presence. Though this is obvious and applicable to everything, for writers in general and poets in most particular, the self investigation of the fossil that is Self is the subject of study. The record of that study is words, is writing, is poetry.

We live in a world and society where recognitions of race, creeds and backgrounds are not supposed to qualify or deny anyone's opportunity for a try at the brass ring. The ever-imperfect world is better for this. But, I here submit that poetry is an area of exception—one where the recognition and display of these precedents is not only acceptable, but is mandatory to the poet's quest. We are: bruised, battered, black, white, yellow, red, ugly, sleek, or beautiful—the record of our pasts. It is our assignment. Truth revealed is not to be shaded or denied.

All would-be poets plow these fields. Some turn clods and grow little. Others, like Carolyn Wing Greenlee, plant, nurture, and harvest poems of beauty, wisdom, and grace. Carolyn has confronted an incredibly complex heritage of race, religion, and clashing cultures; she finds wisdom and strength instead of collapse. She has suffered abusive society and grew up, through, and out. She draws from the inheritance of nature and the shaping of nurture. In both she finds the yarn from which her beautiful writing is knitted.

—*Jim Lyle*
Poet Laureate, Lake County, CA

Preface

In this decade of poetry, I have been processing my life—wrestling my heritage and my past, struggling to understand people different from me. I have faced the fear of loss, the sorrow of watching loved ones age and die, and, in the midst of the worst, have glimpsed the elements required for living fully and finishing well. God continues to surprise me—releasing me from boxes—showing me irrefutably that suffering and hardship can bring about strength, endurance, and compassion. Even death can be a gift if it's committed to His hands.

We are growing up through a dazzling, cold, inhospitable world, but we are not alone; we get to grow together. We are wildflowers—each one different—designed individually by the God of variety. We are to appreciate one another, learn from one another, forgive one another—that we may live free and share our place in the land.

—*Carolyn Wing Greenlee*

Thank Yous

to Bill, whose respect and love for the power of the word catapulted me back into poetry following a sizeable earthquake

Jim, James, Joan, Sandra, Janet, Daniel, Fran, Chris, and the rest of the friends at the Lake County Writers' Workshop who refine my edges as iron sharpens iron, and Dennis, the patient chauffeur

Jillian, who drew me from my cave with patience and gracious lovingkindness

Stephanie and Lynne , whose sisterly support has given me stability and a safe place

my parents, who continue to plant trees

& Jesus, Dan, and Sister Wendy, who, more than any, have changed my artist-life for Good

for Daniel
  who believes in the power of poetry,
  the value of mine,
  & is the best of friends

CONTENTS

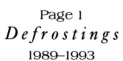

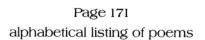

Wildflowers in the Snow

Defrostings

1989–1993

Ten years of harsh legalism had turned this eager believer into a frozen Pharisee—proud of her holiness, secure in her merit, contemptuous of all and anything less. But the Lord of Life had compassion on her, pursued her and wooed her with His "relentless grace." These poems chronicle the first five years of that gracious defrosting.

WE WOLVES
for my sons

We Wolves
slouch low
don't show
soft underbelly
to nobody
but pups
are permitted
invited
desired
to drain
the surge
of milk
and love

FROM LIN FA TO LALU
or From Carolyn To Polly
or To Thousand Pieces Of Gold
From A Buck Ninety-five

Thick shine
      long sweep
            Chinese hair
                  black as ink sticks
                  rubbed fine on stone
                      watered
                  light reflecting whiter
                  against the rich dark
Her eyes
      clear
      do not appear
             slanted
             (the embarrassing adjective
                        shaming me)
My soul
      leaps to hers
            grieves her fears
            chafes her captivity
            groans her indignities
            entwines tightly with her
                  good brain
          her
             fine heart
Forty-five years
      of other faces
      other hair
          curly
           bright
             blonde
          red
           freckled
           blue
          fluffy
        flashy

laughing
　　curved-calved
　　　　heavy-breasted
　　　　　full-hipped
　　　　　　swaying on stiletto heels

　　　　　　　　　　　I—
　　　　　　　　　clumping in oxfords
　　　　　thin sticks terminating in
　　　　　　　　　　Clydesdale hooves
　　　　　dark
　　　　　plain
　　　　　disciplined
　　　　　straight-backed Oriental ways
　　　　　hard
　　　　　as carved teak chairs

Then she
　　(who could have been my father's mother)
　　drew me as a little child
　　called me to live free
　　　　in a wild white place
I embraced her
　　kissed her
embraced and kissed myself
braided my hair like hers,
tying the ends in red for happiness

Thick shine
　　long sweep
　　　　Chinese hair
　　　　　　black as ink sticks
　　　　　　rubbed fine on stone
The wind laughs
　　　　tossing my hair
　　　　　　black brush strokes
　　　　　　　　on wide
　　　　　　　　　　white
　　　　　　　　　　　　sky.

Would Your Father Give You Stones for Bread?

Even if I *could* turn stones to bread
would bites be delightful
or by the second mouthful
turn from grain to gravel
    crushed to powder
  dust of heights
ground down
        Heaven's Wisdom Way
          disrupted
              disarrayed
        dismayed
  and stopped
  by my own clay

The shoot slides up
then the stalk
then the head.
We don't know how it happens
but it does.
The life is in the grain of wheat
that falls to earth and dies.
The patient farmer waits
and is first to partake.

In Time,
    You make all beautiful.
In Time,
    You make Stone edible.
In the hopeless dust of wilderness,
    You are our supply.
Great Stone Rejected by Builders,
    You are our surprise:
        Priceless Bread of Heaven
        Precious Bread of Life

LORD,
I wait
and YOU talk
        Manna from Heaven
        Water from Rock

STAYING

The old covenant
is worth the sweat
isn't it?
Vows are meant
to be kept
not fractured
just because
we're tired
irritated
sore
bored

Depths in your soul
are possible
when you choose to choose
what you chose before
for better
or worse
even when worse
goes on
          and on
                and on

Honor is rare

                Effort
                    the surprise
                    that rises
                    from the heart
                that continues
                        to try
Love roots down
                long
                    well-branched
                    firm-grounded
                because

flowers
are not the only good reason
to stay.

PRAYER FLOWERS

Jesus,
When the enemy is firing
And the fiery darts are flying,
I don't need a friend with flowers,
I need a friend with faith
Who can help me see my Savior
Through the smoke and strange behavior.
Through the lies that boast and tower,
I need a friend who prays.

I need a friend who'll praise,
Who'll remind me of Your power
To keep, secure, and save
Till *my* understanding flowers
With the wisdom of Your ways.

In You

In you
    are whispers of God life—
        traces of Spirit
            like silver trails of snails

      I wish you would
          with a flying tackle
              grab God
                & wrestle
          till your heart was broken
        and loneliness spilled
          to the last
           trickle

ODE FOR TOADS

How can we love the warted ones
With toady ways
And grasping tongues
Who leap with ugly splaying toes
And leave their slime
Upon the roads?

I look for kings in castles fair
With golden crowns
On golden hair
Who never burp or belch or wheeze
Or wipe their noses
On their sleeves.

VEHICLES

You are a Mack truck.
I'm a Ferrari.
You keep rollin'
      over roads that would
                misalign
                 my
               front
                  end

But I can go fast around corners
    a sleep streak
        low
          I purr
You rumble
  reliable
  good for the long haul

I racearoundracearound
    this track
        that track
           pit stop
      quick!

We're traveling the same road
    with some variation.
  Are we willing along the way
    to leave our own vehicles
        to render aid:
          me, a diesel mechanic
          you, with metric tools?

RISK

for John

Deep weeping goes on from a place without time
  abyss of loneliness
    no one can fill
Where is the beauty
  we were told we could have?
    wholesome children
       laughing in sunlight?

Where is the God of my father?
  a certain weight in the silence
     at the fading of the Bach
Where is assurance of order—
Someone wise, concerned, aware?
Why is napalm? cancer? anger?
If God is Life, why so much death?
    dark? despair?

If you will not arise, yourself,
and scorch the evil from the earth,
then I must wage the war myself
and rage against the darkness

I am offended by you
who ordered your people to kill
even beasts and babies
of those who chose not to worship you,
plaguing your children with fire and snakes—
blasting them into terror with your own loud
           Voice

How can you claim to be a kind, loving Father
when your actions
are destruction?

You are the myth of a people
in an ancient distant land,
made up
to explain hardship,
    give meaning to wandering
        reason to the random.
                Somehow it gave them comfort.

I do not need a god like you—
god of blood, disease, and sword.
With shots and scalpel I attack
what you refuse to banish from Earth.

I am disappointed.
Bitterly betrayed.
He told me you were Faithful,
    a place of peace,
    a Rock.
Where is the God of my father?
Where is the God of Bach?

Yet, somewhere, in the thin, clean air,
on a mountain,
You were there.

In the place of deep weeping
    in abyss of loneliness,
        I ache
            I wait
                for
            You.

Upon Reviewing The Former Safe Life

Everything before was quietly orderly,
no one thing overly.
    But now
    they feel flat as a toad on a country road.

ON TRIBAL FRIENDS

If my desire had been to find
another one of my own kind,
I would have worn my best hopes out.
       Now *you*…
       How did He *do* that?

Litter Mates

We are close as litter mates
whumped down
nose to paw
short soft down coats
smack together
eyes shut
sigh
comfort in the other
breathing

This was Dad's idea
not ours
that birthed in us
the same
eager
heart

THE DAILY DIVINE

When you're all together and everyone is well,
it's the trip to Galápagos you recall,
trying to get housing during the War,
how he left you with babies and went off
    gallivanting with friends,

But
when he is gone,
it's the disarray of papers,
the missing irritating wadded socks,
the garbage you must now take out
yourself

Every day is now
louder
slower
crowded with details
    with him
           without

One wonders…
Would it be all right with God
to slip away in sleep
to simply cease to be
because this place
is too empty
&
too full

TRUTH IN THE INWARD PARTS

today, I am abyss
pebble dropped down
   falls a long time
            faint/distant/small/splash
               invisible in black

I could switch the halogens on,
drive that bulldozer
cram space with beams and girders
   heavy construction
         urgent/significant/meaningful/work

but He won't let me hide
                  in any less
                           than Himself
He tucks His majesty inside
                        abyss

SPARROWS

little birds
brown and plain
are not less noticed
than flashing stallions
sea-churning whales
or cool, still herons
       blue
    on
          blue
little birds
fly into windows
lie broken on the roof
while wild winter rains
   scour their feathers from the glass
     and nearly nobody knows
               or cares

a billion people in China
could care less
about our tears
    our deaths

but Jesus sees the brown and plain
broken against the window pane
and recalls the hot sun
and the grit of Jerusalem dirt

BURNT OFFERING

two days before May
i obeyed—
flesh fire
fresh flayed
merciful
holocaust
sparing nothing.

Yet,
piercing ash,
the gentle green spear
blossoms
giddy pink,
cheerfully contradicting
the finality
of
sacrificial
death

For Love Of The Bride

You who designed
    skin to long for skin
    lips that cry for lips
    hips that rivet the eyes…
You who ordained
    love to seek love
    a pairing of spirit
    deeper than all others
allowed Yourself
    not one small kiss
    no fingers drawn across an eager breast
    nor close breathed "I love you"
        from one beloved above the rest.

DEEP THAW

You've had enough
of my Ice Queen routine—
breathe on me
till white begins to clear.
I can hear
small stirrings
circulating red,
murmurings
of nerves
violet and green.

I am afraid
of melt down.
How do I keep
contained
Adam's even now
accelerating?

I collapse
in the heat
but You
catch me
hold me
with arms too faithful
to fail.

Light Works

earth's sweet fire
    is but a moth
   battering dust against the wide pane
                     of Eternity
          Beyond,
            His Voice
        makes the fragrant colors dance
          and the Song goes on
                  Forever

Wildflower Season

1994–1996

When the wildflowers are in bloom, I drop everything, grab my camera and go. For a few weeks, Lake County is vivid with successions of yellows, blues, pinks, whites, and golds. Red larkspur wave from steep banks. Clouds of vetch purple the sides of roads. During wildflower season, everything else is on hold.

Whenever I look at wildflowers, I am impressed with the variety of colors, shapes, places, and times. Some bloom in the shade and only in early spring, some appear abundantly during peak season, and some, remarkably, raise their yellow heads only late in summer in the driest and harshest heat. I am impressed by their opulent display flung lavishly by an extravagant Hand. And I am impressed with how quickly they die.

More and more I am coming to recognize how fleeting are the wonders of this life, but moments, like flowers, need not be lost. Memories hold them in the eyes. Poetry passes them along in bouquets we gather for ourselves. May we never overlook the small, or fail to appreciate the gift of time and one another. It's wildflower season.

AUTOBIOGRAPHY
Inside The Oy Quong Laundry

pieces
too many
   words
   hurts
     unable to tell
     unwilling to tell
     unwise to tell
 phrase
   fault
  scorch
    stop

How to open
without spilling
    my laundry?
    theirs?
My tears
sprinkle memories
spread like wrinkled shirts

Will thoughts
be hot enough
to iron them out
after all these years?

Joy Luck

Is it the way of all mothers and daughters,
   or uniquely Oriental,
the fussy small old lady
with irritatingly immovable ways?

Will I become one?
   shrink & shrivel & snivel
             or chatter drivel,
                  running out my words
                     in trivialities?

I look like the girls in the movie—
   sleek
   advantaged
   cat calm outside
             cat scritchy inside

We are all taller than our mothers,
but they have grit from what they endured—
and because they sacrificed
to spare us from such things,
in some ways we will never grow as tall

On the windward side of the mountains
   in the Aleutian Island chain
   ripping winds assail Sitka Spruce
             which grow close-grained
             prized as sounding boards
             because they transmit most faithfully
                whatever the Master plays.

Walk around Zion, and go round about her,
number her towers
(her lofty and noble deeds of past days),
consider well her ramparts,
go through her palaces and citadels,
that you may tell the next generation
[and cease recalling disappointments].
For this God is our God
forever and ever;
He will be our guide
even until death

—Psalm 48: 12–14 (Amp)

VALUE IS NOT PRICE BUT COST

The old carved box
 with broken hinges
 was never best quality,
        even new,
 but her father gave it
 when they hadn't much
        and now she has given it
                        to me.

TURGOR PRESSURE

Harsh calling
Sleek journey
Will we never flower full?
Tundra petals
blasting the ice night
jaunty in arctic white
Rampaging past
cracks tinier than
craze on a Chinese vase
Forcing into bonebaking day
their fleeting
    fluttering
           dauntless
                Hello

Irrepressible Life
presses from
invincible Truth
valiant in crags and alleys
whole as summer afternoons

SO LONG

after so long
i'm stuffing like a starving man
gulping till i gag
running back for more

i burn
myself
on things too hot to handle
searing my tongue
unstopped by the pain
hunger
only
is real

i want
so bad
to be full
to be full
to be full
i want
so bad
to feel full
whole
real

so long
i've been dead
so long
i've felt nothing at all
the scorch
and the deep deep pain
only mean
i am still alive

i want to live to live to live

i want to live
so bad
i don't care
if it kills me

He Likes Alone Alone

He likes alone alone
He plays his borders sleepless
    flails the past that measures him
    bows to the old lady's curses

My hair is slick black ice
    treacherous on the shadowed grade
    I listen for the gravel beneath his wheels
    and wonder what he did
              surrounded by her fences

COMMON THIEVERY

you can't steal it from me
since i haven't got a thing for you to take.
the warmth at the window you feel
as you hide in the darkness outside
                    is not me

i am as empty as you
        troubled inside with tornadoes of fire and ice
        lurking alone in the darkness outside
                    inside

we are thieves who deserve to die
        but He who bleeds between us
                    Forgives

I Am Not Alone In This

i am
full of emptiness

batholith
with no way out
except an occasional volcano
never fully drained
it
remains
molten
rocks rubbing
deep
       below
             pressure
edges cooling slowly
to stiff black glass
shattering easily
to edges
smooth enough
to effortlessly enter the heart
and stop
cold
any warm life
too close

Thoughts At Three In The Morning

The Arts Council has been shot in the head.

    Did he brandish the gun,
    absorbing her terror
    as a man savoring fresh morning pine?
    Did she fall without a cry,
    surprised to be dying so soon?

and who will take care of her little dog?

It hits hard but slow
    How?
    Why?
        whywhywhy

        wispy dark hair escaping her pinnings
    I see her
    I still see her
    I can hear her
    How can she be gone?

Patricia—
Does it please you
that in this early morning
I am writing poetry
&
in that exercise
I am finally able
to cry
?

Four Weeks After Tina's Death

It seems for awhile
there's a gash
in time

a horrible
rending
rawred

we wonder
how it must be
to wake every morning
and all through the night
hoping
then remembering
then wishing you could
reverse
or erase
or
at least
be also not alive

                    bitter metallic thud trudging days

but wonder wears off
and the rest of us
lark along
hardly recalling
the rip
            so distant
                    it seams

CROSS PURPOSES

For most of our lives,
      we suspect it will come
      but we are seldom prepared
      It is always
            too soon
            too rash
            too harsh
We wouldn't accept it
         believe it
         or yield
      except it happen
      regardless

      too harsh
      too rash
      too soon

To accuse You
         of approving
      ignores the reality
      of Your own harsh death
            our ransom

7-12-94

Mae
Meg
Evelyn
Lillian
each
bereaved
believed
till death do us part
thought
the crowd of days
and slashing edge of sorrow
would mark
her own march
always
&
every
February
July
October
September
every
15
19
7
12
would waft
in every
morning
coffee
Vernon
Malcolm
Milo
George

CONSIDER...

You are generous with sunlight
  gracious with each breeze.
Do encroaching shadows belie that Heart,
  cooling breezes into chill?
The white barked tree stands glistening
  largess of leaves
          once red and umber
                already moldering softly

Hope in the Lord, it says.
Consider the lilies of the field—the birds of the air

Day is destined for evening,
  the only time when other suns show
  and evil must go on a long, long time
Has He not told you?
Yes, He has told me

So let leaves fall
  gorgeous in crisping air
and let go
  your dreams of a better life.
There is no other better life
  you'll see
        you'll see
              but it dreams as it draws its strength
              from deep wet places
              seemingly forever
                until the appointed
                            Time.

CELEBRATION
for Kathy & Nancy

She knew she would be healed
& was
but not
as she thought

You suspected—
brought the children
for five remaining hours

At the end
you sang camp songs
held her hand
poured your love between the slits
into the bit of blue beyond
then fellowshiped her
four last breaths
with three night nurses
you had never met—
standing with arms around each other

you arranged her sosoft hair
curled around her soyoung face
sat in holy early morning peace

                        eternal

                              then

                                    opened the window

FOR JONATHAN DAVID

he
has eyes like apple seeds
shinydark with slumbering trees within
he
scrunches when he sleeps
gruntingsnuffingsqueeking, then softysofty breathing
he
cries effortlessly
producing tone with perfect aperture
a proper projection,
rather than a screechy wail
and
he
goes from full gale force
to slack
relaxed
in familiar arms

he
has mommy's hands
daddy's eyes
a tranquil soul
    & gas
    &
    he
    has sturdy bones
    tiny nails
    silkysilky spikey silky combination red/black hair
        &
        we
        cannot understand
        how one so small and new
        could make us fierce with love and joy
        so soon

10-14-94

ANNA CHRISTINE

black hair
brown eyes
almond shape
no surprise

you look like her
you look like him
you are yourself
and both of them

who you are inside delicate skin
God only knows

but we will love
to help Him
help you out

3-23-95

TO THE CHEROKEE WOMEN

How can we be sisters—
    you who come softly through woods and plains?
I am the daughter of a laundrywoman
    hollering across clothcovered boards
    slosh of wash
    and hiss of press.

How can we be sisters—
    you who mourn your stolen land?
I am fresh off the boat
    a reunited wife
    ten years apart with my infant son
I am a small girl
    turning endless socks
I am Third Generation Californian
    set in the middle of White education
                    getting good grades
                    making no waves
                    not even a ripple

In this hostile place
I did whatever I had to do
    to belong

You were here already
    and still you don't belong.

How can we be sisters?

Until Bruce Lee
with thanks to Bob Boyd

Until Bruce Lee,
every Chinaman shuffled
bobbed like a toy
grinned through oversized teeth.
Until Bruce Lee,
every Chinaman talked funny
acted foolishly
did laundry
and cooked.

Bruce kicked the hell out of lies
(quite literally)
and we were free
from burning shame
from devouring diminishment

Then came Peking acrobats
world champion figure skaters
a tennis player
Lalu
Joy Luck
Gum San traveling museum show
and me.

I THOUGHT THAT WAS ODD

I always felt out of place, too Chinese-flattened face, too
unAmerican girl to be asked out
Then Nixon went to China and Chinese was *in*.
I thought that was odd

Then I wrote for *Jade*, thought is was great—
carted it blithely to Sac State
thinking Asian Studies would like it too.
I heard the term "banana" for the first time
and suddenly I wasn't Chinese enough.
I thought that was odd

Then there was Bruce
and people thought I knew karate
asked me if I always ate with chopsticks
ate a lot of rice
could see my other eye
I asked did I look like I always ate with chopsticks?
I guess I did
to her.
I thought *she* was odd

The kids were enchanted when I talked at their school
crowded around and touched the porcelain
blue and white painted so intricate the design
marvelled at the 5,000 years
juxtaposed
with the scant 200
told me they thought Chinese was nice
and I was the first they'd ever seen.
I told them that all cultures had goods and bads
and Chinese was not better or worse.
I don't know if they understood
but they didn't think I was odd;
they thought
I was beautiful.

I LIKE MY POETRY

I like my poetry.
I am not like the eloquent Chinese boy
still wrestling to please his dead father
              hating his poetry
              feeling always it is not good enough.

I like the stretch of syllables in the spoken word—
the pressure of inflection, dips and pauses.
Is it unseemly?

I like to read my own out loud,
playing with velvet and
the tips of consonants.

Should I be ashamed?

I am poethussy
              shaking my syllables
              flaunting my floribunda
              flashing my
                    well-turned phrase

Should I be embarrassed
              to be so pleased
              with words
              that close with the solid satisfaction
              of a well-made carriage door?

VOICE FROM THE MINES
a prophecy

When you passed,
did you look down from your horse
and see me in my shack of flattened kerosene tins?
When I paused, squatting on the floor,
        bowl and sticks to my mouth,
did you hold your breath?
or sniff to increase your disdain—
        dead fish stink and grease of many past fryings?
Do you think this is the way I am?
I did not come because I am stupid.
I came because I was poor.
When the women come,
when *my* woman comes,
we will bring forth scholars, scientists, statesmen.
You do not recognize in our diligence
        our discipline of patience.
Back home, we carve limestone
and place it in running streams
for the water's own hand to perfect the design—
sculpture for the gardens of our childrens' children.
Can you think that far?

Do you think me less because I
will take jobs too terrifying for you?
Do you think me foolish to die so often, so easily—
in blasts, in freezes, suffocated by snow, by soot,
by poisonous steam and falling rocks?
I am shot to death, scalded to death,
beaten, run out of town. I am burned,
hurled from mountains, dropped from baskets
hanging from a thread where you will not go.

Does it make me worth more
or less
that I will trudge on day after day
to send my pennies home?

I will bring forth physicians, judges, tennis players, skaters, writers,
actors, reporters, painters, 'cello players, inventors, comedians,
singers, politicians, playwrights, and poets. I will astound you with
acupuncture, T'ai Chi, meridian balance, Bruce Lee. With the
strength of patience and the wisdom of restraint, I will invade your
businesses and change the face of your commerce, build houses in
wealthy districts and influence your politics with dignity, reason,
and decorum. My children will take your scholarships and graduate
with honors.

And yours will run the streets.

But I did not come to conquer.
I came because I was poor
and thought
here
I had
a chance.

Wildflower Season

We are wildflowers,
  scattered,
      wind sown
Warm rich meadows are our homes,
ice regions of the North,
sand-washed sullen hot breath plains,
cracks of rocks
  cheerful cascadings
      celebrating roots that hold

We are often
  individually
  unseen
We have beauties known
  mostly to ourselves
We have learned to live
  where greenhouse flowers die,
      We who are vapor ourselves

From the window of a passing car,
we are massing
        all alike
        an array of force and color
        covering the world
From where we sit,
we are each ourselves
        separate,
        but close
        opening and closing
        alone.

We bring delight with variety,
tears
    with the soft yellow dust of our fertility
We are opulent, lush, generous
                                gone
        trusting the rest to integrity of seeds
        and the faithfulness of tomorrow

Senescence

1997–1999

I was wild about botany in junior high—intrigued to hear the answers to my wondering: Why did leaves turn brilliant colors in the fall? Why didn't trees bleed to death when they lost their leaves? And how could the tenderest of shoots grow up through the thick concrete of city streets?

Words floated in dim memory for the next forty years—abscission layer, auxin, turgor pressure. Then, a few years ago, I happened to sit next to a botanist named Barbara who graciously answered my questions during the hour-long flight. Had I remembered correctly? Yes, there was an abscission layer which enabled the leaf to separate from the tree without trauma. Auxin was a kind of plant hormone which caused central growth—root growth. And turgor pressure had to do with the force of fluid against the cell membrane which enabled a plant to push its way up through a hairline crack, widening the gap as it grew.

Barbara surprised me by telling me that the reds and yellows are always present in the leaf, but the chlorophyll masks them until cold weather signals the plant to start gathering its energy back into itself. As the chlorophyll withdraws, the brilliant pigments are revealed. Then she said, "Here's a new word for you—senescence. It has to do with any kind of aging."

It was my fiftieth year. I was having those unsettling shifts in hormones that bring on a host of alarming symptoms including a fear for sanity. I was watching my mother begin a frighteningly fast decline in health. And the society which worships youth and beauty had declared I was officially antique and very nearly obsolete. There were physical, cultural, emotional issues lurking in that mellifluous word, senescence.

What does it take to grow deep at the root? withstand separation and loss without losing hope? have enough internal strength to keep growing towards the light when the way seems barred by impenetrable obstacles? How do we develop the character which, at the end of our lives, shows us to be more vibrant than in all our green years? And, in view of the terrifying spectre of the Future Unknown, can God really turn it all to Good? These are questions I've pondered as I continue to grow in this inevitable, ineffable senescence.

IMMIGRANTS

Water
  pounds
  straight
   down.
 Home lies
 straight up.
 Against such
  rush & crash
you fling yourself
           past rocks
             bears
          exhaustion
           flailing air
             gasping
        iridescence gone
               no glory left
                  save one:
                      this I do
                        for my young

Watching the Super I Max feature, "Alaska," I was overwhelmed by the sight of salmon leaping vertically up a giant waterfall six stories high. How tiny they seemed!—how impossible their task! Battered to shreds, the fish finally reached their destination where they spawned and died. The scene changed to show eggs magnified so large they filled the screen. The narrator said they would develop and grow "in water enriched by their parents' decomposing bodies."

This poem is for my grandfather, his father, and all immigrants who came to the Land of the Golden Mountain seeking to give their children a better life.

WITH ALL DUE RESPECT

"An earlier generation blazes the trail
on which a later generation travels."

前人開路
後人行

With All Due Respect, Sir,
We cannot redefine ourselves
except in disembodied mind.
Forever tales from former trails
remain firmly packed
from countless footsteps
of those who passed before.
Removing
from the continuum,
catapulting ahead
like cosmic time-space leap frog
powerfully disengaging from *chronos* time
is illusory.
We are bundled
in ineffable lines
invisible if you go alone ahead
haunting
as a single silk thread
insistent
as spider web.

Which means you can try to ignore your roots, but they're always
still there and as long as you deny them, they'll continue to pop up
and shock you in compulsive, and sometimes embarrassing behav-
iors. They are waiting, hoping someday to be recognized, not as
bondage, but as belonging.

Thoughts for Jay at 2 in the morning after he said, "You define yourself by the
past; I define myself by the future."

Behold, children are a heritage from the LORD,
The fruit of the womb is His reward.
As arrows are in the hand of a warrior,
so are the children of one's youth.

—*Psalms 127:3-5*

ARROW CHILD
for Jay

the pulling back you feel
is tension that's intended
to propel you
in release
having found your niche
in your line.

57

APPLES AND ELEPHANTS
for Jim

You sit squinting
    loathe to be fooled
        lured
        lulled
           by figments
           bells

You disdain
    flaws
    foibles
    foolishness
    faith as noun

You dissect
    words
    dogmas
        assert
        your own
        having no evidence of things hoped for
           assurance of things unseen

But GOD has spoken to me of stars
    held my heart in sparrowfalls
        whispered hope in blossom boughs
           brought my thoughts to rest.

EDITING IN THREE WORLDS

for James

We sit
side by side
you with blue eyes
studying to retain
your Indin side
me, yellowfaced
Third Generation Americanized

yet these chosen words
arrayed before us
like Long Life noodles
in porcelain bowls
celebrate centuries
rivers
     wisdoms
               dance
beckon to the stranger
bid me enter
see how we differ
feel how we're the same
groping for place
tribe
song

I am proud of who I am
I am proud of who you are
in all hearts Eternity
calls
beyond other belongings

IF YOU HAD BEEN BETTER LOOKING
for Bob

If you had been better looking,
it might have been too easy
to get the girl
who could be won
by looks
alone.
But you were fashioned
for better goals,
harder paths,
deeper walks.
You were designed
with one in mind
who would hear your heart,
value the broken,
recognize the chosen
and rejoice.

PROJECTION

What did he scream
in the long last hours?
        agonies of rage
                at the god who left him
                        to the tyranny of endless years of days
                                bibs and bedpans
                                and occasional casual calls?

When she heard him through the walls
        on her first night there
                she could not have known
                        it would be his last

She knows now
        news trembling ear to ear
        crowding those remaining
                with fears of their own last time

And what will she do?
        scream at the God she forsook for her love
        at the ones who only promised to come
        at the ones who surround her now unnoticed
        blaming the man who left her
                the futility of all those years
                without a drop of satisfaction
                though she wrung them with iron hands

What will she do when the endless days end

and what would *I* do in her place?

MIASMS

what she did to you
you do to me
you can't help it
you go
over the edge
like a stick over Niagara Falls

PREYING HANDS

I am busy, very busy
Spinning hands and spinning mind.
Those who rush to hurry past me
Are just passengers of time.

They avoid the close encounter,
Make excuses for their flight,
Buzzing off to games and meetings,
Claiming distance is their right.

I'm the center. I'm the reason
They are husbands, they are wives.
They should wait on me, their mother.
I've provided all their lives.

Nonetheless, I'm very patient.
I'll endure their evil eye.
Someday I will spring and grab them,
Wrap them tight and suck them dry.

PALL BEARER

A pall hangs over you
as if you are ever expecting to die.
Lest you think it prophetic,
remember your mother had one, too,
and she died at eighty-nine
or years before,
depending on your definition.

OLD LOVE

She comforts him
in his incontinence
has a routine
guides him through it
settles him in the small room
rinses his clothes like diapers
disinfects the seat

Mother As Autumn Leaf

Sap retreats
leaves
wrinkle
drybrittle
bones afraid to fall
riddled with holes
birdlight
and shrinking

She is shaken
but in her shaking
more appears—
flexible
unabashed
sturdy
in beauty
and holding on—

Surprised
I recognize
all the years
under green
she's been living
gold vermillion.
She learned it
in the drought.

LOSING MOTHER

You are evaporating
before my eyes—
you who were
solid as stone.
Your hands
ripped boxes,
kneaded my knotted calves,
gripped reality,
wiped, swept, & chopped
faster than
Yan Can Cook.
Now they tremble
and you tell me
for Christmas you want a bib
with a catcher at the bottom.

You watch yourself
fade
brisk
no more—
takes all day
to leave a chair

I seem
too fast.
I should be less.
I have always been less

but you're the one
diminishing—
bones like glass
fingers
wind-ruffled grass

IDENTITY CRISIS

I have always been
　　　strong enough
　　　　　to meet head on
　　　　　whatever comes—
By sheer will,
　　　able
　　　to wrestle
　　　　　trouble
　　　　　　　to good.
I had no time
　　　for petty pity—
　　　　　by necessity
　　　　　rising from
　　　　　infirmity
　　　　　to wait on those
　　　　　　　less disciplined
　　　　　　　than I.
It was my job,
　　　my duty,
　　　my destiny,
　　　my calling,
& again & again
　　　I climbed
　　　impossible cliffs
　　　to accomplish
　　　what had to be done
　　　　　lest there be lack
　　　　　or insufficiency
　　　　　in any way
　　　　　　　for those I love
　　　　　　　and serve.

But now
    they wait for me,
    wait on me
    rub my back
            my feet
            my hands
    bring me pills
    sweep the floor
            where pieces of dinner
            fall

I used to be
    fast
    efficient.
Now everyone else
    is more so

& I grieve
    that I cannot
            protect them
            do for them
            give to them
                    as they now
                    do for me.

I have always been able.
Now that I'm not,
I'm not.

CHANGE OF FUTURE

When days thin to basics,
the future no longer stretches out
a seductive song
enticing and inviting—
it drags by
stripping
as we once pulled plums
from summer branches.

Always Never Coming Home

Distant siren
fading day
say
They're never coming home.
I am twelve again.
I am nine.
So many nights
in front of the window
watching for headlights
listening for tires
as long as I remember
they were always
never coming home

I am fifty-one
mother of two
grandmother of three
president of a corporation
chairman of the board
I have written books
spoken before many
sung before crowds
traveled plenty
I have been a grown up now
much longer
than I was a child

yet in the failing light
as distant sirens fade
I am twelve
I am nine
and they are never coming home

LARYNGITIS

Today,
without my voice,
wanting to speak
and nothing will come,
I know how you must have felt
in the old days
before you knew English
and even after—
even now
when laughter is loud
and mocking—
even now you flinch
though it's been more than
seventy years
and you have long made peace
with childhood fears.

MOTHER'S LAMENT

When you shook with fever
I held you
sat all night rocking
greased your raw bottom
mopped up your vomit
sang away your terrors
smoothed away your fears

When you married outside wisdom
I stood by
cried
when you couldn't see

When you had babies
I made you broth
strong rice wine and ginger
celebrated first month
red eggs and *licee*

All these years
I've carried you
in my mind
on my back
How can I help?
What do you need?
All these years
I've loved you
How can I
be the one
who hurts you?

licee: money given in small red envelopes.

73

MOVING VIOLATION
Rape And Thereafter

uninvited
velvet chestnut skin
i watch
descend
    my friend
       no more

    too numb
    to scream
      my brain
      guillotined
      by disbelief

        i am not here
          and forever after
             i am not
             here

SOUTHWEST FLIGHT 541

We take for granted
    lift of wing
    engine drone
    cool air hissing
        directional
        adjustable
Olympians,
    we glide over peaks
    that stopped hearts
        and wagons
            cold
    forests
        reduced to moss
    rivers
        threads of web
            catching light
        which formerly flexed secret eddies
        sucking transgressors down

If this cabin were suddenly to lose pressure
    yellow masks to fall
    metal obeying
        gravity
        not
        lift,
we would find ourselves small
ground large
hard
and next breath
most consuming
but now
    tray tables down
    seats back
    ice clicking
        we remain
        murmuring
            nodding
                expecting
                    Nothing

INCARNATION
thoughts at 32,000 feet

From cloudlevel
serene order
silence

why would You come
close enough
to hear cries
look into eyes
souls
sin
?

You put Your feet on Earth
and let it get
under Your skin

Two Widows
on flight 458 to Ontario

It was bizarre
sitting between those two
both in their seventies
both widowed one year
husbands contractors
who thought nothing of driving
those thirty-foot motorhomes
they now had to sell
for far less than their worth
because they couldn't
handle those things
alone.

Both had lots to do
with their lots of widowed friends
exercised regularly
lived in lovely houses
missed their husbands barely
reveled in their freedom
carried photos of terriers
instead of grandchildren.

I sat
hearing of doggie antics
my wallet crammed
with pictures of grandchildren
too young to disappoint me
to the point of carrying
photos of my Labrador
instead.

POINT OF VIEW

Down here
there are walls & thorns
spikes & towers
immovable objects
boxes

Down here
ants big as submarines
roar away
clutching food
I've stored for winter—
spiders seal me
in cabled cocoons
sucking my nectar
to dust

Up there
You tell me
it's not a box
it only looks like a box

Up there
You tell me
You're my tower
Bread for winter
Eternal River
nudging deserts
into
sweet full plums

Look
up here
You say
Wait
& remember
for love
for you
I swallowed
dust
spikes
thorns

NOT KNOWING WHEN TO LEAVE
for Vince Moses

Today
I was not *toong hey*.
Forgive me.
So long I have not seen myself.
So long I have cringed from public eyes,
            voice low
            so not to draw hearing to my face
            dropped gaze
            if sight stopped on eyes of unfamiliar man.

I did not know I had kinsmen here—
            thousands—
            once there were thousands.
I cannot tell you what it means
            to know they nursed the first two trees
            then washed, brushed and packed
            the overflowing orange gold

It was not for them

but for me
this knowledge comes
now
seeing their headstones
            soy sauce pots
            broken bits of glass
                        carefully swept
                                    from entombing earth

I was not *toong hey*
        because you longed for those men
        sought their names and lives
        wrote them in a book
I who have had no voice
        could not stop telling
        because you asked
        because you wanted to know
I who have had no face
        have seen it
        in theirs
                even here
                where I grew up
                never seeing a trace

My fault
in truth
was not
not knowing
I was staying too long on the phone,
keeping you
past the end-drop in your voice,
my fault was staying anyway—
not *toong hey*
for joy

toong hey: lit. *clear air*. Means doing things right, operating with propriety, being sensitive to the comfort, needs and schedules of other people, *i.e.*, knowing when to leave.

For Annie

You dressed
in Chinese red—
   no trace of blue
   to subdue
      the *yang*,
but Western-style—
   no mandarin collar
   regally concealing your throat
      though you sat
      like a queen

You were a knockout
in the days you vexed your mother
   never at home
      jeeping over boulders
      without roll bar or belts
You're a knockout still
   at 86
      mind bright with memories
      of the way it was
      before houses, gangs, and stroke
         reduced available space

Now you can't go
except with cane
   slow
   who loved to gallop in halcyon hills
   swim, run,
   have fun

How would it be
to have accepted one
of the blue-eyed boys
who ran with you?
The comfort of sons?
Even your dog is gone.

You still see much,
but sharp and sour now—
    overbusy lives
    avoiding penetration.
You only mean to help.
You only want to give
    a car
    a house
    advice
    wisdom of nearly a century

What good are they to you
to keep to yourself?

    Will they end up uncashed checks
        among the litter
            after 50 years?

What is the sum of those halcyon days—
the meaning of messages your strong mind has mulled?
You who were never home
now never leave
unless someone stops by
saying, Come with us, Annie.
Annie, please come

You berate
your difficult body,
wonder how you got this way.
You were meant for open spaces,
    laughing friends,
    cantering in the wind

FOR ANNIE 2

I see my mom
in your handsome glance
still guarded
from wounds
from second grade.
In my hug
you are stiff,
but pleased.

BOK FAHN
In Honor Of White Rice

Plain *bok fahn*,
fragrant steaming—
Taco Bell can't
set me dreaming.
Every kernel,
pure and sweet.
Lox and bagels
can't compete
with innocence
and soft demeanor.
Who'd prefer
a salty wiener?

Meek, supportive,
self-effacing,
willing so
to be the spacing.
Curry chicken,
broccoli beef—
too much flavor
needs relief.

Gentle *bok fahn*
clears the tongue,
setting, gemlike
every one of
sweet and bitter,
salty, sour.
Soong has praise,
but *bok fahn*, power.

bok fahn: white rice
soong: the other food

85

WESTWARD WOMEN

Westward women
   weren't always willing
      but love
      or fear
            pressed them to beginning
            from the spot called
                "Independence"

Westward women
      weren't the same when they arrived
      as the ones they started out
      as the ones they left behind

Westward women
      buried husbands under trees
      left their china in the dust
            by castoff wheels
            broken by ruts
                by jostling and pounding
                    by parch
                    by scorch
                    by snow
                        drifted high and holy white
                            covering cattle
                            standing hollow
                            covering bellows
                            growing weaker
                            old and younger
                            growing weaker

                    hunger held them helpless
              and boredom trudging step by step
        counting dangers
      two thousand miles

Westward Woman
   figured out
      how to fix a dandy meal
      over buffalo dung
      they selected themselves
         no longer worried
         about spoiling their hands
      tried to describe
      with words too small
      what only Overlanders saw
         spire stones
         prairie dogs
         yellow orange lace
         under water smelling foul
         prairies so flat
         nothing stopped the wind
      mountainsides so sheer
         they broke your heart just to look

Westward Woman
   made love
   babies
   home on the range
   rinsed their dried red rags
      discreetly
      (when there was water)
   kept their woman-hearts
   discarded all the rest

When Westward women arrived
   they had learned to improvise
      set up new lives
      in split skirts
      riding astride

knew they were strong
could do a man's work and
not be one
having driven cattle
battled bugs and varmints scuttling in darkness
and snakes

Westward women
couldn't wonder anymore
what folks back home would think—
they had become
Women of the West
and couldn't explain
or have to.

Hospice

days seem full & empty
too much time & not enough
                wanting to be together
          needing to be alone
            torn by too much
                    & too little
              & missing…
        already missing…
            wishing it were over
            yet dreading the day
                  when things will never
                  be the same

                        forever…

THE AMERICAN WEST

The American West
has long attracted
encouraged
rewarded
prized
  I can
  I will
  Nothing ventured, nothing gained
  He who hesitates is lost
  No holds barred
  Full speed ahead
    all *yang*
    no *yin*
      which is where I
      come in.
  You say
  When in doubt,
  floor it.
        I say
        Look before you leap.
        He sins who hastens with his feet.

      You are red–haired. I have black.
      I whisper caution. You attack.
      In terms of partners, our balance is best:
      My Great Wall crossing your American West.

REVERIE

You are a very talented, irritating person.
I wish I could get along without you.
If you were gone, my life would be simpler,
but not better,
except I could go back to thinking
what a good person I am.

Sudden Blows

Sudden blow
out of nowhere
so hard
blue marks come.
You were doing nothing you knew of
to warrant it.
She had warned the class
three times,
Whoever is humming, Stop it!
You were writing "O's"
unaware it was you

She asked me what I used to say
that made her so mad she would hit me.
I said I didn't know,
but it was probably something,
knowing me

Now we strike each other
sudden blows out of nowhere
warranted by warnings
for things we're repeating
unaware.

REALITY

You told me you were not a nice person.
I did not believe you.
I believe you now.

I thought I was a nicer person.
Now I know I'm not.
We've known each other's hatreds,
      glowered dripping with each other's puke
      shocked by our own violence
           ashamed

Others looking upon us
think we're such nice people.
Are we always uglier
      the closer we get
 or were we like this
      all along?

COMFORT ZONES

You dive in.
I hesitate.
You beckon.
I follow.
        Water rushes into my ears
           blurs my eyes
            closes over my head
        Frantic toes search for solid
              find none
I flail to the top
      gasping

With easy strokes
        you're yards away
I am thrashing
        drowning
You wonder why I'm crying
        babbling paranoias
            phobias
                fears
you, who are terrified by
        clowns
            crowds
                certain formations of clouds

LIKE THIS

It isn't you, you know.
I would have been like this
all by myself
except I wouldn't know
I was like this.
I would be like this
with anyone
I depended upon
was afraid to lose
was afraid I'd drive away
if he got too close
and saw
I am a trainwreck.
But you are a trainwreck too.
Almost nobody isn't
though most people never get close enough
to find out
or stay together long enough
to find out
it's okay.

I Now Know Why Brokenhearted People Write So Many Cryinyourbeer Songs And Poems

They're trying to explain
to ears already gone
what elicited the pain
and what the hell went wrong.

We Like The Dance

We like the dance
of each other's thoughts
intricate
original
no worn-out plots

Of course, the very unpredictability that we enjoy in not being able to anticipate the steps predisposes us to some bruised toes and accompanying ill-feelings, but it's really nothing personal—just the nature of our natures. If we didn't dance together, we could sit back and enjoy each other's genius, but we'd never experience the exhilaration of two minds moving as one.

I Think We'd Best Stay Friends

He brings me peppers
fresh picked today,
glossy and green
from the garden
he plants and tills himself.
Brings me supplies
from far away—
fifteen years he's done it.
No problem.
Glad to.

He cans his harvest,
vacuums his car,
balances his checkbook
to the dime,
changes his oil,
shampoos his rugs,
brings his Bissel and
shampoos mine.

In fifteen years,
I've always had his ear,
a sympathetic word
Scripturally based.
In fifteen years,
we have never
had a fight,
thought the worst,
made a fuss.
In all my life
I've never known
a more affable
comfortable
man.

But we still live three hours away,
don't see each other every day
or have to bear each other's gall
or fear the risk of loss
or walls
or jealousies
monsters loosed by intimacies...

I think we'd best stay friends.

FOR LACK OF EQUUS
or Where Is Monty Roberts When We Need Him?

You are a flight animal
    fearing fences
    kicking ragingly
        any unexpected rail
            you might bump
            on your blind side
    any enclosure
        seemingly
        closing in
What slap or whip
    cut you till you
    tolerate no rules?
What omnipotent woman
    rode you
    till you refuse
        orders, meetings, regular hours
        authority: anathema?

You drop your head for no one.

Your mustang feet
    hard as the stones you run on
    spatter away from the beaten path
        the pastured way

Big empty skies are your reward
vast blank plains your domain
    nothing to impede
        catch your foot
        saddle
        or
        bridle
        your
        sensitive will

There is a perfect language,
each sign meaning just one thing.
If I knew it,
you might hear it

But there are unseen rails

                I bump and kick,
                musts, shoulds,
                violent words,
                fences I must flee

Vast blank plains are my domain
                silence

                    refuge,
                    my reward

SABBATICAL

7 years you've loosed your
wild dog words on me
    shot your arrow looks
    blamed me for your excesses
7 years I've thought
    if only I would stop doing
    whatever I'm doing
    to trigger the fury
    everything would be all right.

My fault has been
    paralysis
    peace at any cost
    throwing steaks to appease the dogs
    taking flint in the guts
My fault has been
    believing
        love meant no fences
        limitless like Indin lands
        without boundaries or lines

I have spent my whole life
accepting the harsh boots
of anger that belonged
to someone else.
I have taken the blows
as mine—
owned,
deserved,
warranted by some invisible, inflammatory flaw
that would inadvertently inevitably signal the dance
I could never prevent or avoid.

Today I am
a cur
ribs still sore from the last time
snarling and waiting
sensing cruel music
overtones wide and low

Will I accept your hateswung boot
whimpering and cowering
confirming your contempt
or rip you red with
my own wild dogs?

After 7 years
I've had enough.
It's time for the land to rest.

PULLING UP STAKES
for Jillian

you beat me
i don't remember
though it was years
they told me it was years

you raped me
twice
because you said
the first time
you came too fast

you blame me
seeing all your disappointments
frustrations
unrealized dreams
feeling thwarted
it must be my fault

you revile me
thinking I try to put you down
make you look bad
you do that just fine
all by yourself

you use me
convenient slime
to beat
fuck
kick
blame
having your pleasure
at my expense

I see you, Pattern:
I have been the elephant
resigned to the stake,
believing its grip
more than the Lord
Who says
>You are My daughter
>cherished
>beloved
>apple of My eye.
>I did not die
>so you could live this way.

Today
I realize
I need not stand here
anymore.

ALL THINGS WORKING TOGETHER

After I flayed you skinless,
laid out in 12 pt Helvetica
what I hadn't the Presence to say,
I looked at the print
and you were not there—
only thrashings
misunderstandings
words heard
dimly
through the static of our
other lives

You were not angry,
only hurt
that I wrote
revile.
You said you never meant to.

I believe you,
remembering
contradictions
of descriptions
of blood
and boots,
remembering
I have torn you
and not meant to.

We have been through
lifetimes of clouds
memories of dreams
and broken things.
We have grown up
through cracks
childhood lacks,
filling in blanks
with gifts of ourselves.

Inside me now are solid fences,
clear lines,
true ground.

Inside you are breathtaking open places—
Jesus working
in the Wild.

POETRY IS CHEAPER
AND MORE CONVENIENT
THAN A THERAPIST

I love poetry.
It does not argue
contradict
belittle
interrupt
interject
or
blame.

Conversations in my head
go around and around
never ending
just justifying
logic more watertight
and more vitriolic.

But poetry
surprises me
soothes me
with cadence
and just the right word.

I pick through
debris
of fires
blasted trees
brittle gray ash
finding clues
finding hope
finding reason
for life again.

TERRITORIAL RITES

I am not your territory
so please stop peeing on my foot.

PARTIAL PARALYSIS
Reverie After Half An Hour In A Dental Chair

Ice jaw
foreignfrozen—
if I bend my lip,
I can't feel it—
only the slobber on the right
and suspicion
that even more
is on the left.

Humiliating
not knowing
when to wipe,
wondering
whether smiles twist
grotesque.

My hand
feels warmth
from my chin.
My chin,
indifferent
feels nothing—
odd
uncomfortable
nopain
alienating,
uncaring.

I am impatient
rejecting
wishing to escape
this dead thing
that is half my jaw
realizing
with guilt
my shot
will wear off,
but others live
years
with ice
where their faces
should be

SNAKE CHARMER

He
rears up
spreads his hood
obsidian eyes
unblinking
pierce me to the bone

His tongue
quick and narrow
twists to logic
whatever suits him best

He slides
so effortlessly
the ground seems moving
instead of him—
I fight for footing
my ground sliding
when he's around

His words
force me
past conscience
reason
common sense

Shivering
to flee
but standing
still
receiving
the poisoned bite
ice runs swiftly
my heart
freezing
my eyes
cold
watching you come near
I rear up
spread my hood
wait
unblinking
poised with
poison

WHEN YOU WERE WRITING POETRY
for Linda

In 1977
when you were writing poetry,
I was getting divorced
having left my husband of eight years
and two little boys
ages: too young
to have to fight
up out of
the whole I left them in

the Masters
lay unclaimed
for want of
one small volume of
well-wrought verse

I couldn't have written anything,
not even the heavy immensities
of early poetry
exposed in cool sans serif type
forever evidenced in
one thousand copies
perfect bound
black
thin

You gave your disclaimers,
handed me the book

I read the words—
yes, they were young,
but while you were writing poetry
I was getting divorced
abandoning sons
writing nothing

Hard Copy

Hooray for Hard Copy
that my flurry of renaming
cannot erase
that no drive crash
obliterate.
Hooray for white paper
unobtrusive
20#
having still
on its inexpensive
innocent soft face
words I could not replace
or even recall.
For all the spectacular ease
of changing works
without trace of past
to retrieve
from trash
or
binary memory
leaving only
the Best,
I thank the Lord
for paper proofs
not yet burned
destroying evidence
of imperfection

Just remember, any unfinished business with ego development that you missed out on in the eighth grade will come back now. You're just finishing up the other end of it.
                              —Christiane Northrup, M.D.

THANK YOU, DR. NORTHRUP

So that's why
his junior high
braid-pulling antics
annoy me
fulfill me
help me feel real
whole
where holes once were—
I, too thin
to be seen
too self-absorbed
to hear other pain—

Forty years later
God sent me
someone to
teach me how to
throw rocks
not like a girl
and tease me—
he sees me
doesn't think
I'm too thin

To My Granddaughter,
Now Three Months Old

Meghan Kathleen
still unseen…
my son says you're placid
like him—
soft dark hair
calm dark eyes
familiar as
months of gazing
twenty-nine years ago

I hold you
weightless,
your face
on his memories
as Grandfather's mother
held my mother—
the Kathleen
she'd never seen

3-18-98

.

To My Newest Grandchild,
Still Several Hours Off

Today
we'll find out
who has been kicking
and giving your mama fits—
messing with her digestion,
keeping her from sleeping.
This morning
before light
you entered my life
through the voice of my son
who hiccupped and somersaulted
 through my ninth month
even in such confined space.

I love you already,
prayed before you were conceived
that you would be
all that God delighted
to create
of cells
spunk
spirit—
heritage from your tree
of pioneers
from three countries
and a long, hard way.

Your parents
tried to take
a sonogram peek,
but you kept to yourself
these long months—
the unveiling

now perhaps
many grueling hours ahead.
They are worried
but happily
believing that you,
unknown even as to gender,
are worth the pain
you will cause them
the coming hours,
years.

I agonized decades
that my little Chinese acrobat
with eyes like drops
refusing convention
would catch his foot
jumping over or off—
break his neck
and my heart.
He has never
done either.

You,
uniquely twined
gift of insistent genes—
long desired
much prayed for
cherished child—
still remain
to be seen,
revelation
pursuing
a lifetime.

6:37 a.m.
11-16-99

For Grace Elizabeth

Dear Baby Grace
only 30 hours old,
when you are 30,
I'll be 82.
You shall think of me
as a very old granny indeed
and be amazed
that I know so many things.
It's from living long
you know.
You shall also know
much more than you do now
when you are as old
as I will be
when you are 30.
For now
your little blank brain
is snapping arcs
leaping across space
with not much network branching
highways faster than a speeding bullet.
You know nothing of
autumn,
the splendid time
when all Earth changes to vibrant clothes
to celebrate
in honor
of
your birth.

11-17-99

DARING BEHAVIOR AT 4:00 A.M.
or This Is A Typical Symptom Of Peri-Menopausal Women, So Don't Be Alarmed; I'll Get Over It
or This Is A Typical Symptom Of Peri-Menopausal Women, So I'm Not Alarmed. Get Used To It

If I'm gonna be awake in the middle of the night,
I might as well get up and write.
In the darkened room with one light on,
I reach for rhymes to word my song.
It's a new thing:
Making music when I can't sing.

Melodies inside my head,
Rhythms thought, but never said.
Oh, what would my husband do
If he knew?

Morning comes and I'm a zombie,
Blurry-brained while doing laundry.
Worse at work,
Worse yet by evening—
Talking backwards, scrambled reasoning.
Can't adapt,
Or take a nap—

But it's been so long since I've tumbled in delight
Melodies and lyrics in my head at night
Or any songs in any way…
People have to choose their poison,
Passions, pits, and what annoys them—
Pay the price or else avoid them.
Tomorrow
I will pay.

RED

Red used to be
The color of hussies
Scarlet women
Scarlet letter
Scarlet O'Hara
Red light district
Cardinal Sin
Flagrant
Flamboyant
Immoderate
Red
Immodestly flaunting
burning shame

Red was to me
The color of alarm
The color of No
The color of Stop!

Today
before the mirror
I liked the color
against my hair
Firecrackers crackling
New Year's night

What joy in
red egg
one month
child!
What hope in
red silk
bridal
gown!

Shame has no place here
no alarm
only hopejoy
Red

INVENTORY

After 52 years
I finally feel
like a grownup—
kitchen-efficient
mostly on time
trauma & lessons
coalescing
in meaningful whole.

It's good
this place
somewhere between
upward climb
&
downhill slide—
success not as sweet
failures not as deep
Life having familiar shapes
faces
friends.

All my life
I've looked forward to
finally having arrived.

For just a little while
as bones begin to dry
sight darken
thoughts wander
I'm going to revel
in this wonder
I have
become.

AFTERNOON DELIGHT

It doesn't seem right
to be writing
while other folks are working.
Shouldn't I be
cleaning house
paying bills
folding laundry
baking something—
maybe muffins?
How can I sit
ensconced
in this
room of my own
with the lake lightly fogged—
soft late sun
delineating curves and trees—
poems tumbling
keys to screen.
I read
satisfied
pleased
blessed

Surely someone will soon appear at the door
tell me to quit fooling around
get back to work
stop wasting time

no one comes
and still
I feel guilty

Song Of The Sparrow

I won't ever get a Grammy,
Oscar, or an Emmy.
Pulitzer or Nobel Prize—
Not likely I'll get any.
But I'm content to write my books
And sing my little songs,
Wash the dishes, feed the fish,
And try to get along
                with others.

To be unknown is not the same
As being a nobody.
Fame can make a man a pain
And arrogant and haughty.
The privacy which fame precludes
Is just my cup of tea.
I'm glad to have my peaceful, quiet
Anonymity.

The problems that I struggle with
Are ordinary ones:
Dennis, Daniel, menopause
And insufficient funds.
It's not likely I'll be stalked.
Super model I am not,
But I am pleased with what I've got
And thrilled where I belong
When all my normal, ordinary,
Sparrow days are song.

MUSINGS ON ONE OF THE FINAL FEW

Hot red river, and plenty
nobody's taking up residence there
in the old apartment
glad to still see
evidence of fertility
though not as faithfully
as before
glad to know
estrogen still flows
her appointed rounds
greasing bones
not yet riddled
brittle
curving
off course

My mother says
she never had time
to fuss about
The Change
too busy
never noticed any
swings of moods
always crabby
anyway
just dried up
that's all

Some say
I'm entering
my wisdom years.
Some say
I am
over the hill.
Chinese say
living longer
makes me
venerable
honorable
valuable
respectable.
It's good to be Chinese.
I like it more
each year.

ANNIVERSARY TWENTY-ONE
for Dennis

I appreciate you,
patient as an ox
treading out grain.
The stable may be messier,
but much is the gain
from a man who has lived civilly
responsibly
devotedly.
Duty is your
modus operandi,
harmony,
your goal.
You were born
in more orderly times
decades before
Anything Goes.
It has been hard for you
to live with a woman
who runs her own company
all over the country.

Your mother set each place
with full service at each plate:
knife, two forks, spoon

even when all you had was soup.
(One time you told me
I had to do that too.
I remember.
Do you?)

The blending of lives and expectations,
tastes and generations
is harder than people imagine,
but better,
if it happens.

Twenty-one years
we've worked our ways
and stayed.

Together
we've modified
each other
for better
or worse
for richer
or poorer.

We decide.

"Why are you bringing this up?" they said.
"Why don't you just let it be
water under the bridge   *You replied, "Do Jews forget the Holocaust?*
passed, forgotten   *Do Japanese forget internment camps?*
silent as bones   *Do Blacks forget slavery?*
crushed under stones   *Do Indians forget broken treaties?*
never retrieved…"   *Chinese are the only ones*
     afraid to remember."

BREAKING SILENCE
for my father

Why must the Chinese be made silent by old fears
when many voices
are speaking now of the terrible times
and America is finally ready
to possess its unedited past?

It is not for blame we speak now—
not to complain
or make ashamed.
It is to remember
and honor.
It is to learn
grieve
and not repeat
lessons of history
accessible only
if we are willing
to face
and tell
the Truth
without blame
without trying to make ashamed.

210 Freeway
In The Pouring Rain

Slow it down
she tells him
rain obscuring
the written road
fast cars passing
spray clouding
alarm
adding to
already hostile
hurtling
slick grey
air-colored
our car-colored
rain-covered
road

I
backseated
imagine often
frantic sliding
slamming
silent
wonder
if today
I'll regret
to die

PERSPECTIVE

I read her my poem about crashing on the freeway.
"What horrible thoughts you have!" she said—
she,
who tells me about Nazi torture,
bodies of horribly emaciated prisoners
slung naked over shoulders
of unconcerned guards,
violent house invasions,
Road Rage.

She
likes action movies—
things blowing up
the louder the better,
kung fu fighting
lots of high kicking,
bad guys spinning
off roof edges—
screaming all the way to
sudden stop.

I guess
it's knowing
that movies are makebelieve
and atrocities happen
to someone else
appearing only
as print
in the paper
or news
on the screen
at six o'clock and ten.

But death in a car
on the freeway
in the rain
is not only possible,
it's prophecy.

We've waited
for the screech of doom
all the years
of commuting,
all the years
of picking up and dropping off
and shopping—
we've waited
weeping at the window
for headlights to turn in,
or the phone to ring
and the voice to say,
"They're wheeling your father away."
He told me that once.
I've never forgotten.

It doesn't help
that in the seven days I've been here
he's nearly run off the road
the hapless cars on the right
twice.
Fortunately,
there weren't any villains in them—
glove compartments stuffed with guns,
cussingly chasing us down,
Road Raging us
to oblivion…

FROM THE PLACE OF THE POOR

For Jonathan, living in Pomona
in honor of two generations who came before

Father,
you grew up
in a concrete world
dust of city
sweating your brow.
One small fan
was all you had
to cool your
hot harsh labor,
steam reddened skin,
days without end

You longed for spaces
acres untended
places
impossibly green
and giving

When you had money
you moved
to a far place
where we could gaze
all day
on sky and hills,
flowers cascading
from carefully randomed
plantings,
baskets hanging,
terraced slopes
coaxed into color.

I grew up
not working,
not knowing
concrete
sweat
dust
sleep like death,
but your tales
drew me
like dreams
to the center
of your strength,
source of your conclusions,
burden of your past.

Your weight bearing
exercised your soul
till you rose
a giant
in my eyes.

Now
I must return
to that concrete world
to gain
from ancient memories
what you and your father earned—
to draw
from this place of the poor
what Jesus said
was Good.

Internal Combustion

when you two fight
I feel my own civil war
yin against *yang*
yang against *yin*

where is the yielding?
the leading?
the perfect balance
of broad and focused views
acquiring and preserving
fulfilling in one?

dark/light
left/right
wrong
the strong
is meant to
strengthen
the weaker
is meant to
soften
the hard-line
one-way
short-view
do-or-die

We must
harmonize
lest this terrible noise
rip our subtle union
past mending

I recognize
your opposing forces
vibrating in my bones
twining in ribbons
patterns so old

the rest of my soul
has settled over them
layer after layer
sediment stone
marking floods and droughts

your obsidian edges
cry to my
hidden glass
made molten
then cold
then cracking open
upheaval
revealing
bands
dark and light
easily eroded
and unyielding
still unmixed

I see
the stark
uprising
despise
my own
fracture
distrust
my own
guidance
arguing
both sides
without
resolution

ENTROPY

He says she's getting more and more like her mother.
She says he's getting more and more like his father.
Always the worst parts thereof,
this deleterious deterioration.

Behind fretful accusation
prickles apprehension
that the monster parts
of longdead people I don't know
will overtake them both

He's diluting the soup.
He's diluting the soap.
Whatever we plan,
he changes—
logic perfectly rational to him,
incomprehensible to us.

Her frustration
increases
as facility
decreases.
Don't ever get old she says,
quoting her mother.

His father, a miser.
Her mother, a shrew.
In my old age,
shuffling and deaf,
will I, by Christ,
escape the Sentence,
or
locked in DNA
end my days
cranky
stingy
irritated to the core?

HOWLING AT THE MOON
for Csimu

I envy you
red brother
whirling in dust
wailing in dance
howling at the moon

I sit before fire
hear wind
blast trees
drive
small soft raindrops
hard
against cold glass

I am sheltered by
this strong house
how long?
are there no
lactating mares
comforting the night
of silent wolves?

If I had your
Talking Stick
I'd clutch it
till my hands numbed—
unremitting rush of words
blasting this
somewhat secure silence

then
we would see
what remained
while I stalked through darkness
howling

GUARDIAN MOTHER

You are Guardian
Keeper of Good
Harbinger of Doom
Watcher at the Gate.

Vigilant
you admonish:
      Be *toong hey*
          not stinky fish.
    Don't spend all your money.
          drop names.
          ask favors of your friends,
              using them as stepping stones.
    A promise made is a debt unpaid.
    Always take a gift
          and write a thank you
          right away.

Inspector,
you invested your rich life
in the three of us
      making sure we had lunch,
      oral hygiene,
      coats if it looked cold outside.
Inspected,
we labored
      to chop the right way
          (fingers curved,
          knife against knuckles,
          never stupidly
          sticking out nails).

You scrutinized
our expressions
            correcting exaggerations
            excesses.
We must always be
                        exact,
                                    never redundant
                                    or rude.

Your Standards
are irrefutable
having been established eons.
Even weak as you've been,
nothing escapes
your accurate eye
            with or without
            an unclouded lens.

You pounded
endlessly,
your rod of commonsense
impacting dirt
till particles
wouldn't dare part, sheer or shift—
            no abrupt avalanche
            mudslide
            erosion
            subtract from the foundation
            you gave your life to save.

To this day,
I cannot bear
a buxom blonde babe
scantily clad
swooning in her hero's arms,
adding her one hundred-twenty-pound
voluptuousity
to his already harried escape.
To this day
I hear,
"Stupid female! Get up and run!"

Today
I rest on solid ground
moral,
responsible,
carting gifts
writing thank yous
pained by my inaccuracies,
        discrepancies
        redundancies
never fainting
        until after the crisis—
chopping
        somewhat stupidly,
        sticking out nails.

toong hey: lit. *clear air*. Means doing things right, operating with propriety, being sensitive to the comfort, needs and schedules of others.

Artisan Father

Where you are
is
on the edge
    boldly going
    where no one else
        would ever even think to go.

When you are ON,
    you work your magic
    and walls come tumbling down.

Your magic works
    on everyone but us—
        immune after decades
        to spells
        and twinkling.

No one is Stranger for long.
No one is safe from your charm.
Flashing, dancing,
    you know how to make
    the biggest splash
        diving in
        with both rash feet.

You heed no danger.
Accept no obstacle.
Enjoy the difficult
and often the impossible.

You have dragged us all
across the whole United States
more than once,
carted us to Canada,
parked by a spring
in early morning,

knowing
      that's when big horn sheep
      come to drink.

I have admired
      your derring-do,
been dazzled by
      your dashing heart.
If there's a risk,
      you take it
      never counting the cost—
          leaving that
              to Mom.

You know how to romance us:
      roses in every room,
          a big one for Mom,
          buds for your girls.
You check our oil,
      fill our tanks with gas,
      monitor our tires,
      bring around the car,
      warming it inside
          lest we shiver
          even a little.

You have taken us to malls
and never complained about time,
stopped at museums of every kind
read all the signs,
kept us in books
and shoes,
asked how an ugly guy like you
could have such pretty daughters—
still open doors,
offering your arm

You have sung to us
My little girl, so pink and white,
even though we were brown.

You have made a big to-do
of every birthday
one week long—
suitable regaling
for daughters of the king.

You can ignore us
run over us
insist,
resist—
unmovable
unreasonable
incomprehensible
crushingly implacable

You are infuriating
exasperating
frustrating
mystifying
magical
inaccessible—
you are definitely
inevitably
yourself.
No matter how irascible,
you've got your style.
Your life
is one continuous
creative act
and even you
have no idea
where you're going,
nor do you care.
It's always new
adventure—
always
the perfect day
to go.

PERFECT MATCH

When you married,
did you know
he would be the kite
and you would be the string?

When you proposed,
did you suppose
you would need her ropes
to drag you from the swamp?

She has spent her life
keeping you from flying off,
hanging on desperately
to your ascending legs,
surprised to find herself
aloft.
You have spent your life
opening caves
with magic words
dragging her into
radiant worlds
and places of terror
from which she's
helped you escape,
having checked out
on the way in
all possible routes
suitable for a hasty exit
should one be required
(which one most certainly will).

She continues to warn
after nearly sixty years:
Watch out for that car!
Take an extra coat!
Don't you hire that guy!

You listen
sometimes
and sometimes
you turn off your ear
when she tells you she told you
    when he doesn't show up
    day after day.

                    She knows these things,
                      she tells you.
           She can feel them ahead of time.
                And she's right.
                    A lot.
                  And also
                        not.
      But she doesn't remind you of those

I didn't understand
(though you both said the same)
    that cutting tones
    and flailing words
    were just your way.
        I'm a cloudchild
        easily pierced.
            All those years
            I got in-between
                didn't stop the strife
                or soften the blows,
                though I took them
                as my own.

    You are both of earth,
        sensible
        practical.
    You complain,
        get loud
        get hurt.

She recounts every fault
time, place, and detail.
You assert
shift blame
defend
And when decibels reach
a specified level,
both of you simmer down,
never resolving—
never agreeing—
both your wills
and points of view
intact.

And sometimes
you are frighteningly one:
concurring on
the need for guns,
the hostile state of the world,
the impending economic crash.
You both believe
partners
are a bad risk
and friends can become
worse than enemies.

You agree so completely
that you feel as if you're
only one person—
so consistently
that I feel at times
you must be right

I finally understand
that you love each other,
your fights are not fatal,
and you're not going to get a divorce
after all.

I finally feel secure
that your union
is a good one—
not an uneasy truce,
but a solid state.

I recognize
I am your blood
your values built
into my bones,
your histories,
your legacy—
my inheritance

I am also Father's child
with a whole different view
from a whole different place.

We are farflung flowers
various and vital
pulling color up
from the soil where we grow,
enriching earth
in our fullness of days—
each voice
valid
with its own
enduring song.

Autumn Sparrow
upon seeing her photo for the first time

Today, I look upon your face.
I have not seen it since the Sixties
when I was a college girl
driven in a car at night
through unfamiliar streets
to look into a coffin
at a stranger.

It was you,
my father's mother.
When I was one year old,
you came to see me.
I don't remember.

My father rarely spoke of you.
I grew up
never missing you
who had gouged
a hole in his heart
when he left
without hearing
tearful entreaties,
without seeing you throw yourself
across the door,
pressing a small
bone-handled dagger
to your breast
protesting his going

All broken hearts
have remained till today—
no recognition

melting stone shards
to river together
gold and red
heavy flowing down smoking mountainsides
building up layers of themselves
by mere passing

Today,
I look upon your face
smooth
well-shaped.
You were the beauty
sold at four.
You were the scandal
bearing two men's broods

I have not cared about you,
but lately
I've been missing you,
watching you move
through the pages of my father's book—
watching you more
within boxes and walls,
shuttling back and forth
depending on who was where—
depending on whose you were…

I began to long for you
complex, mysterious woman
thinking fast
caring hard
landing on her feet.

WING SONG

It's Papá.
I mold
my voice
to Pleasant—
ends of lines
attentive upturned faces
awaiting his words

Add Mamá
on Speakerphone.
   She sounds far away—
      rattle of pages—
         she's reading news
            talking to me
            talking to him

I ask her to speak up.
She does
   for awhile
      then drifts off

They drift off a lot these days—
   no longer holding
      all reins tight

He is tired,
   voice frayed
      soft shop broom shuffle
         where once were solid words

I can't get used to hearing him old.
He was never old.
Never walked old
till he lost his toes—
striding in his 70s.
Now he says, "Go on"
    and sits
    while we walk the mall and back.

'Course,
he's always made a friend
on the bench—
    learned their troubles,
    offered them hope.
        They are sad to see him go.

I am sad to see him go,
though he's able at 83
to bind a box tightly
packed to the brim
overweight at the airport.
I have to remove
soy sauce and canned bamboo,
hoisin and dace fish tins
lightening the carton
he loaded alone.

He seems younger than she.
She says he made her old—
resting while she foot-ground herbs
    he the scholar, she the farmer
    (she says it gave her great legs, though)

I remember
she spent her life
juggling it all—
office,kids,husband,home—
hostessing
          with style,
          only trembling
          the last
          3 years.
Now she's losing ground,
not heart,
still elegant
still wanting to be part of it all

so fast it's come
so fast it's gone

If they had not been Something,
there would be nothing to miss.
I flinch from the wrench
as they're whispered away

They tell me, "It's warm"
so I'll know how to pack
for the week I'll spend
          trying to break the heartbreak—
                    keep her company
                    keep him corralled
                              in the book we're doing
                              on their life.

I wish I could tell them
how much I miss them—
    who they were before
    who they've always been
Now I guard her in parking lots
    as she once guarded me
and he naps
    while I correct his paragraphs

They still work early.
I drag myself from bed,
peek outside the window
    watch him tractoring
    her inspecting squash.

I'm thinking:
I am both of you.
I have your genes, your loves.
I'll grow old like you—
finding friends on benches,
valiant in dust.

FOO GUA

Ever since I could chew food,
my mother has been trying
to get me to eat
    and like
        foo gua.
"It's good," she said.
She lied.

I took an unsuspecting bite
and wanted to spit it out—
except that's unacceptable—
so I gagged it down
and drank a lot of water.
"It's bitter!"
"But afterwards," she smiled,
"it's *herng*."
       She looked very wise,
           knowing Greater Truth
           beyond the immediate,
           attainable only by discipline
               and great cost.
I wasn't willing to pay the price
      herng or no *herng*.

Fragrance afterwards,
      that's *herng*,
but I would rather avoid
      that first assailing shock
      revulsion
      and extensive effort required
      to suppress
      what comes up.

Sixties Child,
   born under the burden
   of the powerful Red Button,
   I skirted every murmur
   which might lead to War,
         kept silent
         lest I draw fire,
               rapists,
               lions in the streets.
I was afraid
      to speak up
      or out
      lest I be shot
            up
            or
            down.

I have lived dishonestly
      ignoring the terrorists
            howling in my head
      afraid to let others know
      how I really am
            or what I think of them
            lest they decide
            I'm too *foo gua*
            without any payoff

Whatever made me think
I had to pay off?
What am I?—
a slot machine?

Life is *foo gua*,
       inevitable
       bitter
       bumpy
       shiny
       intricate
       deeplyplumply
       green

I can expect to meet
       the unjust
       the ugly
       the violent
       the cruel

I can also expect
       perfume in my mouth
       fragrance
       enduring
       well past
       pain.

foo gua: bitter melon
herng: fragrant aftertaste

GOD IS NOT OSTRACIZED FROM SKILLED NURSING

Old hymns stir pictures in old heads.
"Once we were young with so much to do!"
No one complains about them now,
forcing Church from State.
"If it comforts them,
slumped slackjawed in their chairs,
let them sing,
let them pray.
It doesn't matter.
Why should we bother?—
their God of Commandments
can't constrict them
anymore."

ROAR OF THE BOAR

Roar pours out from *dan tien*—
Can you stop it?
Most unlikely.
I've had to sound pretty
too long.
False lives
only smile.
Men can rant
cuss & strike.
Women must avert their eyes
soothe
create peace

I've never been a screamer
even when I had my babies
never been a fainter—
stayed in harness
mute as an ox on the Oregon Trail
doing duty
because that's what oxen do
If there is work, let's do it.
If there's a lash, endure it.
On a rocky narrow ledge
take no offense when they
yell at you because your foot slips.
Oxen notice nothing.
Deserve nothing.
Get nothing
but dust in the throat
trudging the ruts and waste
of all who go before.

I was not born in the Year of the Ox.
I am a wild boar
tusked and fierce
broad in front for pushing through obstacles
narrow behind for fast escapes

Mother was not pleased
with the sequined phoenix dress
symbol of the Empress
passive
yin
hemmed in
by custom
expectation
tradition
never questioned

Mother was a rebel child
speaking truth
taking
as the price
the beatings it returned.
She never conformed to
satisfaction
with gowns of
simpering satin—
she wanted
The Dragon.

I am the voice she never had,
one generation more—
I will risk for both of us
Scream of the Dragon
Roar of the Boar.

dan tien: the body's vital energy center located just below the belly button

MONOLOGUE WITH GOD AS AUDIENCE

I enjoy talking
to myself
so much
that I don't want to
make space to
listen to You.
There's always a lot buzzing,
several channels I can change to
if I get tired of any one show.

People say they like my talk.
I smile
warmly satisfied
that Your wisdom
passes my lips.
I forget
those wisdoms come
in the worst of times
when I'm cowering behind some couch
hoping nobody
moves the furniture.

Today,
I began to see
my plaid patterns
crossing at right angles
boxed and squared
around and around
no way out.

I've been telling You
all the troubles
artistically
articulately

having none of the
comfort of Your lap,
Your Daddy arms
holding me away
from clear and present dangers
which are only real and ruinous
if they're all I believe.

You who chose the last gasp
of summer leaves
to flurry in scarlet and gold
know how to transform
winter's bleak crush
to fluttering
giddy
multicolored spring.

In view of
my view of
grind
wrench
and tear,
all my conjectures
disasters projected
calamities
tragedies
and harbingers of doom
I think
I've said enough.

Your turn.

RETURN TO SENDER
with gratitude to Sister Wendy

When did I start believing
the committee in my head
that said,
"Get a real job"?

When did I stop remembering
He sent me into the weeds
to learn to see slowly
recognize the lovely
in the unlikely
and take pictures
so others could see too?

When did I stop
loving my work?

When did it become work?

I who prize
        the words
        the eyes
had lost
        the reason
        the passion
        but for one
        unabashed nun
        willing to revel
        because God wanted it
        for all
        for all time
        for all humanity
                is meant for better
                than a real job

SINCE YOU'VE BEEN ILL

Since you've been ill,
      my whole life has changed—
not just the multiple trips
      400 miles,
           or the trips to stalls
           wide for wheelchairs
               where we laugh about how I now
               do for you what you did for me—

Since you've been ill,
nothing's the same.

I drive my sure-footed little green car
and wonder about my own ease
      turning the wheel,
      feel of curves
      smoothly banked.
Once you drove 120 miles per hour,
      passing mile markers every 30 seconds.
Once you flew the Lincoln,
      taking a turnpike curve too fast.
This morning,
      I was behind someone slow.
      I remembered how six years ago
           you drove slow
           unsure of the edges.
           You almost nicked a cyclist,
               who let you know
               in no uncertain terms.
           You drove me to the mall
               and to church,
               even though you didn't Believe,
        because I was going blind
        and you thought it better to
        drive
        yourself

than to ride in terror
seeing all I was missing.

I no longer take as my right
    the ability to fasten buttons
    tie my shoes
    comb my hair.
I no longer take as guaranteed
    my ability to stand
    walk
    or control my bowels.

I think of my health now
    in terms of
    temporality.
I think of you
    in terms of
    temporality.
We always are,
    in reality,
    but always
    in the past
        it only murmured—
        a fearful possibility
        rehearsed since
        I was a child.
    Now I wonder
    if this will be your last
        and how I can bear
            to be without you—
        how I need to hear your voice
            however small
            sense the lifelong link
            now connecting us
            woman–to–woman.

You taught me
    the sweetness of adversity

Shakespeare
and toads.
You have bought me enough warm coats
to last the rest of my life.

Your suffering
        has made me the one
        who now listens
                through fears
                and scary new losses,
        forcing me ever nearer
                the matriarchal throne.

If I didn't know there was More,
if I thought this brief, hard life
        was the sum of the meaning
        and the totality of time,
I would be sorry
        that you had so many oppositions
        when hugs would have been a better gift.
I would regret
        the toil,
        bemoan the few
        dear
        delights.
I would complain
        that you must end
        your eight sacrificial decades
                plummeting towards
                Absolute Yin
                        weakened
                        stripped of
                        your few pleasures of
                                competence
                                books
                                and good food.
If it were not that we know
        God can change even the worst

                    to the best,
          and that you will be
                    satisfied
                    beyond belief
                              now that you Believe,
I would be much sadder
          than I am now,
                    though I am sadder
                              than I want you to know.

We have
at the end
of this fifty-three or so
year-relationship
more of what I have always wanted
than all the other times
when you were strong
          competent
          and right.
That's how I know
          God will turn even the very end
                    to the very best:
                              He's already made this
                              That.

Alphabetical Listing of Poem Titles

About the Author

Carolyn Wing Greenlee is a Third Generation Chinese Californian. Her great-grandfather came to California in 1874 to help build the railroad that connected the northern and southern ends of the state. In 1899, her grandfather immigrated on false pretenses, the paper son of a merchant. Her mother was born in a laundry in Merced. Carolyn's father was born in Lodi, his father an herbalist/acupuncturist, his mother a Chinese slave.

Carolyn grew up in Claremont, California, and, having been forbidden to become an artist, graduated in comparative literature from Occidental College and took her graduate work in creative writing at the University of California at Davis. Since then, she has had a number of teaching jobs, mostly teaching art.
In 1986, she founded Earthen Vessel Productions in order to produce music which would not be compromised by the pressures of the Industry. The company has now expanded to include books and videos.

Currently Carolyn runs the monthly writers' workshop through the Lake County Arts Council, has photo and painting shows at various galleries and museums, lectures on the Chinese in the Gold Rush, and writes and edits books. She visits her grandchildren whenever feasible, and lives as quiet a life as possible with her husband Dennis and her dog Velvet in Lake County, California.

Earthen
Vessel
Productions

For Kelli,

My friend from VNA —
If caring is curing, the
grand help given to the
Harwell family gives me
joy and hope. Please en-
courage your young friends
to plan their families.
I have counseled hundreds
of women, even a few men.
That generation needs help to
understand.

Jim Nwall Harwell
603-526-7668.

Facing the Population Challenge

Wisdom from the Elders

Edited by
Marilyn Hempel

Blue Planet United
Redlands, California

ISBN: 978-0692212271
ISBN-10: 0692212272

Published by Blue Planet United
Blue Planet United is a non-profit organization that helps people make connections between three defining issues of the 21st century: population stabilization, sustainable consumption, and the preservation of wild landscapes and seascapes. We create print publications and educational films, along with website resources that foster awareness and action to save the last wild places of this tiny blue planet.

Visit us at www.blueplanetunited.org and www.populationpress.org

Blue Planet United
PO Box 7918
Redlands, CA 92375

All photographs licensed from Getty Images

Designed by Julian H. Scaff
Typeset in Gill Sans and Garamond

Contents

Contents (continued)

Acknowledgements

First and foremost, many thanks to the authors who contributed to this anthology, for their selfless generosity in sharing their ideas and experiences. Obviously, this project would be nothing without them.

We are indebted to our funders who made this publication possible. Special recognition goes to the Morris S. Smith Foundation, Sterling and Larry Franklin, Trustees. Individual donors play an important role. To all of you, a heartfelt thank-you.

When it came to the actual making of the book, the artistic and technical talents of Julian Scaff were essential. Without him, the finished book never would have seen the light of day. Conscientious proofreading was provided by Marilee Scaff and Sally Seven, loyal supporters and friends of Blue Planet United since its inception.

This book began with an idea tossed back and forth between my husband, Monty Hempel and myself. He deserves special recognition for his unflagging enthusiasm and unending support.

The Art of Living
by John Stuart Mill

There is room in the world, no doubt, for a great increase in population, supposing the arts of life to go on improving, and capital to increase. But even if innocuous, I confess I see very little reason for desiring it. The density of population necessary to enable mankind to obtain all the advantages both of cooperation and of social intercourse, has been attained.

A population may be too crowded, though all be amply provided with food and raiment. It is not good for man to be kept at all times in the presence of his species. A world from which solitude is extirpated is a very poor ideal. Solitude, in the sense of being often alone, is essential to any depth of meditation or of character; and solitude in the presence of natural beauty and grandeur, is the cradle of thoughts and aspirations which society could do ill without. Nor is there much satisfaction in contemplating the world with nothing left to the spontaneous activity of nature; with every rood of land brought into cultivation; every flowery waste or natural pasture plowed up, all quadrupeds or birds which are not domesticated for man's use exterminated as his rivals for food, every hedgerow or superfluous tree rooted out, and scarcely a place left where a wild shrub or flower could grow without being eradicated as a weed in the name of improved agriculture.

If the Earth must lose that great portion of its pleasantness for the mere purpose of enabling it to support a larger, but not a better or happier population, I sincerely hope, for the sake of posterity, that they will be content to be stationary, long before necessity compels them to it. It is scarcely necessary to remark that a stationary condition of capital and population implies no stationary state of human improvement. There would be as much scope as ever for all kinds of mental culture, and moral and social progress; as much room for improving the Art of Living, and much more likelihood of its being improved, when minds ceased to be engrossed by the Art of Getting On. Even the industrial arts might be cultivated, with the sole difference, that instead of serving no purpose but the increase of wealth, industrial improvements would produce their legitimate effect, that of abridging labor.

Hitherto it is questionable if all the mechanical inventions yet made have lightened the day's toil of any human being. They have enabled an increased number of manufacturers to make fortunes. They have increased the comforts of the middle classes. But they have not yet begun to effect those great changes in human destiny, which it is in their nature and in their futurity to accomplish. Only when, in addition to Just Institutions, mankind shall be under the deliberate guidance of Judicious Foresight, can the conquests made by the intellect and energy of scientific discoverers become the means of improving and elevating the universal lot.

John Stuart Mill (1806 – 1873) was a famous British social and political philosopher. His works include books and essays covering logic, sociology, economics, political theory, ethics and religion. Among his most famous works are the books *A System of Logic* and *On Liberty*. He was an early and strong advocate of gender equity and women's liberty, writing the essay "The Subjection of Women." Mill's belief that the majority often denies liberty to the individual drove his interest in social reform, gender equality and labor unions. He is remembered as one of history's greatest thinkers. In 1848, when "The Art of Living" was written, the world's human population was just over 1 billion people.

Introduction
Wisdom of the Elders
by Marilyn Hempel

In 2013 Dr. Al Bartlett sent a message to his friends and colleagues saying, due to cancer, he had only months to live. I was shocked into awareness that many of the people who have spent their lives working in the population and sustainability field are elders, with all the wisdom and wealth of experience that the word "elder" evokes. We need to gather that wisdom before it is too late.

I contacted fifteen giants in the field, and asked them if they would be willing to write an essay in response to the question: "If you could assemble the world's leaders in a room and address them, what would you say?" In other words, give us your best advice. All fifteen answered, "Yes! Indeed!" Al Bartlett, with only days left, wrote: "Every government needs an Office of Common Sense. But don't venture in there until you understand the arithmetic of population growth."

Additionally, I asked these elders to share their biographies, their life stories, including why they decided to work on population issues. Each came to their conclusions through a series of experiences and evolving knowledge about the unintended consequences of growth.

I entered the field through a series of "aha!" moments, not by design. I was an art teacher who cared about animals and nature, living in my hometown in Southern California. It was obvious just by looking around that the place where I grew up—the open space, the native plants and animals, the freedom for children to experience nature—was rapidly disappearing. Wild places had almost entirely vanished, schools were becoming more crowded, traffic more jammed, and air more dirty.

When I was born, the world had 2.5 billion people.

In 1993, I attended a speech by Bob Gillespie, President of Population Communication, where I learned that I was feeling crowded because it *is* crowded—world population and Southern California's population will likely triple in my lifetime. Human numbers and activities, resulting in deforestation, soil loss, biodiversity loss, and climate disruption, are stressing the Earth's life support system. He went on to talk about family planning as a solution, and the successful door-to-door services that he had set up in various countries. He explained the importance of education, improving the status of women, and especially developing societal support for family planning.

At the end of the evening I approached him enthusiastically saying, "This is really important. I want to work on population issues." Bob replied kindly, "Are you sure? Almost anything else you can think of will be easier." But I was both naïve and stubborn. I started the *Population Press*. In 1994, I attended the International Conference on Population and Development in Cairo as a journalist. I returned fired-up and full of confidence that the world would embrace family planning and the empowerment of women. At the first speech I gave, a large determined woman marched it, plunked herself down right in front of me and announced loudly, "I have four children. Which two do you want me to kill?" Well, I had been warned.

In 1994, the world was nearing 5.7 billion people.

Today, twenty years later, the world has almost 7.2 billion people—and the United Nations keeps revising its population projections upwards. Maybe there will be 9 or 10 billion people by 2050. Or 11 billion. Maybe. Way beyond the 2.5 billion people who were here when I was born.

How many people can the Earth support? At what standard of living? Asked another way, at what level of consumption? According to the scientific research of David and Marcia Pimentel, at a U.S. standard of living, the planet can sustainably support 1 to 2 billion people. At a modest European standard of living (which is far more efficient) maybe 3 billion people.

Paul and Anne Ehrlich put it so clearly, "The problem is simple:

too many people consuming too much stuff." But when we delve into human behavior, it gets complicated. How can we get from here to a sustainable future? That's the question these essays are addressing.

These 15 elders are the people who follow in the pioneering footsteps of Margaret Sanger, Marie Stopes, Clarence Gamble, Alan Guttmacher, Dr. Charles Lee Buxton and Estelle Griswold. Some of them were trained by the pioneers. These elders are members of the generation that was, in the words of John F. Kennedy, "tempered by war, disciplined by a hard and bitter peace, and unwilling to witness or permit the slow undoing of those human rights to which ... we are committed today at home and around the world." Perhaps that is why they are so driven, so tough and so active—even into their 80s and 90s. They are not sitting back in their rocking chairs. They are the people who keep me at work.

There are strong themes that run through these essays: We stand on the shoulders of others. Thousands would be better, but a few dedicated people can make a difference. Human beings follow behavioral models; therefore we should model the behavior we wish to see. It doesn't take special training—we can all be leaders. Be brave, be strong, but do not forget to have fun. If women do not have reproductive rights, they do not have equal rights. The lack of equal rights causes a great deal of pain and suffering and death. Destruction of the environment, destruction of natural systems and destruction of biodiversity also cause a great deal of pain, suffering and death. Today's economy is based on fossil fuels, but those fuels are finite, and therefore cannot last. Furthermore, the burning of fossil fuels is causing climate disruption, a serious threat to food security, the very basis of civilization.

If you have ever asked, "What can I do?" ask no more. These elders did not give in to feelings of helplessness; their life stories are inspirational. Their essays clearly lay out the great challenges of the 21st century and provide many ways we can work to overcome those challenges.

Humankind has dawdled; it is late, but not too late to bring ourselves and our cultures into harmony with nature, and thus assure a sustainable future for ourselves, our grandchildren and for those yet to be born.

A Chinese proverb tells us: "The best time to plant a tree was always 20 years ago. The second best time is always today." Begin here today.

❖

Marilyn Hempel is the Executive Director of Blue Planet United, a non-profit organization dedicated to helping people make connections between population stabilization, sustainable consumption, and the preservation of wild landscapes and seascapes.

For the last 20 years, she has been the editor of a news journal, the *Pop!ulation Press* (www.populationpress.org). A committed environmentalist, she has embraced the slogan "no matter what your cause, it's a lost cause without population stabilization."

Having lived and worked in developing nations and studied population issues for many years, she believes that the interactive problems of overconsumption and overpopulation must be addressed in industrial and developing nations alike. They are also intertwined with the empowerment of women worldwide.

Ms Hempel participated in the United Nations International Conference on Population and Development in Cairo, September 1994, and also attended the United Nations International Conference on Women in Beijing in September 1995. In 1999, she was part of a UNFPA-sponsored delegation that inspected family planning clinics and social services throughout China.

In 2008 she received the prestigious Paul Harris Fellow award from Rotary International, in appreciation of significant work toward the better understanding and friendly relations among peoples of the world.

Marilyn grew up in California and in East Africa, where her father was Chief of the Social Research Section of the United Nations Economic Commission for Africa. She holds an M.A. from the Claremont Graduate University, an M.Ed. from McGill University, and a B.A. from Pitzer College.

WORLD POPULATION GROWTH

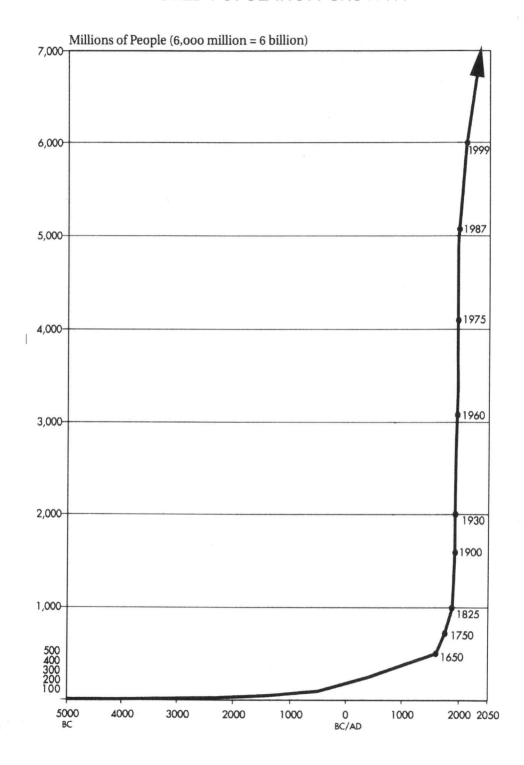

Millions of People (6,000 million = 6 billion)

If I Could Assemble the Leaders of the World in a Room

by Albert A. Bartlett

"Sustainability" has become a key word in our society these days. By its very definition, "sustainability" has to mean "for a period of time that is long compared to a human lifetime". The trouble is that if you look around you, you don't see a very good general understanding, or practice, of the concept of sustainability. Many influential people are confused and think that you can have both growth and sustainability or "sustainable growth". What the heck is going on?

Well, the first thing is that in no way, repeat, no way, is any "world leader" ever seen reciting the Laws of Sustainability, let alone thinking of putting them into practice!

The two simple basic Laws of Sustainability, and how to put them into practice, are not taught. The First Law is that population growth is unsustainable. The Second Law is that no one can sustain growth in the consumption of resources forever. The Earth has a finite size and finite resources. These are laws of nature and they are based on arithmetic. They are not debatable. They cannot be amended or repealed by legislative bodies. Any arguments against these truths of nature are, as Shakespeare would say, "a tale told by an idiot, full of sound and fury, signifying nothing."

Instead of accepting the assertion that growth is both good and inevitable, we should instead focus on the question of *why* should we have more growth.

This is my challenge to you:
Can you think of any problem, on any scale,
From microscopic to global,
Whose *long-term* solution is in any *demonstrable* way,
Aided, assisted, or advanced, by having larger populations
At the local level, the state level, the national level, or
globally?

Every government needs an Office of Common Sense. But don't venture in there until you understand the arithmetic of population growth (or exponential growth). The world's governments urgently need to curb population growth, which is directly determining our rates of resource consumption and our rates of environmental destruction and global climate disasters. This office would also lead the effort to find renewable sources of energy and keep us from exporting the precious fossil fuels and natural resources we have left.

Most importantly, we need to educate our citizens on the absolute Laws of Sustainability* and their importance in everyday life*!*

Read Al Bartlett's "Laws Relating to Sustainability" in the Documents section of this book.

Albert A. Bartlett - In Memoriam
From the University of Colorado at Boulder

Professor **Albert A. Bartlett** passed away on Saturday, September 7, 2013 at the age of 90. Professor Bartlett had a transformative influence on science education and public policy. He joined the faculty of the University of Colorado Department of Physics in September 1950 as an assistant professor, and served on the faculty until his retirement in 1988. He was an active Professor Emeritus until his passing.

Before his scientific career, Al worked as a dishwasher and night cook on iron ore freighters in the Great Lakes. He did his undergraduate studies at Otterbein College and Colgate University, earning a B.A. in Physics summa cum laude from Colgate in 1944.

Dr. Bartlett joined the Manhattan project in July 1944. He worked at Los Alamos studying the properties of the plutonium to be used in the atomic bomb. In 1946, Al was assigned to photograph the atomic bomb tests at Bikini Atoll in the South Pacific. One of his favorite stories is how he shipped home the silk parachute left over from a magnesium flare he used to test the photographic equipment. His wife Eleanor used the silk for her wedding dress, which is now at the Los Alamos History Museum.

Professor Bartlett earned his Ph.D. in Physics from Harvard in 1951, working with Ken Bainbridge, who had been a leader at Los Alamos for the engineering and testing of the atomic bomb. Al's thesis project involved the design and construction of a double focus beta-ray spectrometer. A beta-ray spectrometer he designed and built was installed at the CU Cyclotron in the early 1960's.

Professor Bartlett was one of the most revered and successful teachers in CU's history. He taught introductory physics to generations of young scientists and engineers. He won the Distinguished Service Citation, Robert A. Millikan Award and Melba Newell Phillips Award from the American Association of Physics Teachers, and served as the society's national president in 1978. He gathered numerous other teaching and service awards during his long career.

In the 1960's, Professor Bartlett was one of the founding members of PLAN (People's League for Action Now) Boulder, a citizens group that successfully limited housing growth on the mountains above Boulder by setting a maximum elevation for city water. Boulder's pristine mountains, city parks, bike paths, greenbelts, and open spaces are the direct results of Professor Bartlett's leadership.

Dr. Bartlett is world-famous for his acclaimed public lecture on "Arithmetic, Population and Energy". This lecture highlights the irrefutable connection between population growth and the energy crisis, and provides a compelling call to action. He gave the lecture 1,742 times in forty-nine states and seven foreign countries. The lecture, available online on YouTube, has been viewed nearly five million times! In his lecture, Professor Bartlett concludes his argument as follows: "The greatest shortcoming of the human race is our inability to understand the exponential function..." His advocacy for zero population growth and protection of the environment was tireless.

I. Family Planning and the Empowerment of Women

The Roads Not Taken
by Malcolm Potts

World population has tripled in my lifetime, not because women are having more babies but because more children are surviving to reproduce in the next generation. Tragically, the extraordinarily successful global effort to reduce infant mortality was not matched by a similar effort to make family planning universally available. The classic description of the demographic transition occurring because couples have fewer children as they become more educated and rich is being replaced by a greater emphasis on the role of access to family planning as the essential driver of fertility decline.

I have just returned from an international meeting on family planning in Addis Ababa attended by 3,000 people. I heard very few things that could not have been done 20 years ago or even earlier. Using poet Robert Frost's words, what were some of *The Roads Not Taken* because family planning was not more widely available earlier in the 20th century, and which could have changed the global demographic trajectory?

Augustine or Pelagius

In fact, the first divide in the road was theological and it was 1,600 years ago. The Adam and Eve myth equates sex with sin. St Augustine (354 - 430) went on to crystalize the worst possible interpretation of human sexuality, arguing that Original Sin was transmitted from Adam onwards in human semen, like a latter-day AIDS virus. Celibacy was the ideal and the only way to justify something as evil as intercourse was by the need to reproduce. Pelagius (390-418), a Celtic theologian, emphasized individual autonomy and contradicted Augustine's misinterpretation of sex as Original Sin. Had Pelagius's road been taken, today's world would be a much happier place.

Brock Chisholm or the Vatican

When the WHO (World Health Organization) was put together after World War II, the first Director General, the Canadian gynecologist Brock Chisholm, assumed that the work of the organization would include birth control as well as death control. But Augustine's dark teaching persisted and Belgium, Lebanon and Greece asserted that "to introduce contraceptive methods to underdeveloped peoples was tantamount to giving them weapons to commit suicide." In the WHO corridors Vatican representatives threatened to destroy the new organization and set up one of their own unless the WHO stopped talking about family planning. Family planning was pushed off the WHO agenda just as population growth rates were rising. It was a road not taken that may well have caused more unintended pregnancies than any other missed opportunity in the twentieth century.

Rei Ravenholt or Jesse Helms

With the WHO blocked, a few leaders like Gen. William Draper began lobbying the U.S. Congress to set aid money aside for family planning. Rei Ravenholt, a public health physician, was appointed to run the new program in USAID (United States Agency for International Development). The work was perceived as controversial, but instead of being deterred by finding himself in an isolated position, Ravenholt created astonishingly successful family planning programs in many countries from Brazil to Indonesia. Even Mathew Connley, the most vitriolic critic of international family planning agrees, "Ravenholt's office was virtually alone in its policy of refusing support for programs to create demand for contraception. He argued that supplying 'unmet need' would be enough to solve the problem of population growth, or was at least worth trying before trying anything else." Ravenholt saw safe abortion as an intrinsic part of family planning and began making manual vacuum aspiration equipment available.

In 1973 Jesse Helms, the Republican senator from North Carolina, passed an Amendment to the Foreign Assistance Act prohibiting the use of funds for the performance of abortion "as a method of family planning." Taking the Helms fork in the road condemned countless women to death from unsafe abortion and slowed the progress of family planning across the globe.

John Rock or Pope Paul

John Rock was the Catholic obstetrician who conducted the first clinical trials on oral contraceptives in Boston in the 1950s. It tells us a lot about the history of family planning that when he began his work, contraception was still illegal in the state of Massachusetts. It was also the time of Vatican II, when the Catholic Church was looking to reframe its mission to meet the realities of the 20th century. Pope Paul VI established a Papal Commission on birth control. Despite attempts to pack the Commission with conservative cardinals, it concluded that The Pill was a licit method of contraception. But in 1968, Pope Paul wrote the encyclical *Humana vitae* rejecting this advice. He returned directly to the teaching of Augustine that the only justification for sex was procreation.

Had the Philippines been allowed to take the road not taken, then like Thailand, it would now have replacement level fertility and the people would be much wealthier and better educated—and not have 600,000 unsafe abortions each year.

Lord Flory and Lord Rees

These two presidents of the Royal Society, London, are emblematic of the glacial pace at which the academic community has handled something as profound as population growth and access to family planning. Howard Flory received the 1945 Nobel Prize for his work on penicillin. An open-minded Australian, he understood both the threat of burgeoning population growth and the power of family planning. As president of the Royal Society, London, he created a working group which he hoped would make evidenced-based statements on population and family planning. Tragically, Florey's vision ended with his untimely death in 1968.

There was half a century delay before Lord Martin Rees, also a president of the Royal Society, set up a similar working group. It issued the *People and the Planet* report in 2012. I was the youngest member of Florey's group and one of the older members of Lord Rees' group. Global population more than doubled during the half century before the correct road was taken.

The Roads Not Taken

If it was possible to track human misery on the surface of the Earth with the accuracy we can measure carbon dioxide in the atmosphere above, then a reasonable case can be made that the bishops, popes, patriarchal legislators, and all who closed the roads to ready access to family planning almost certainly brought more suffering to the world than Genghis Kahn, Adolf Hitler, Joseph Stalin, and Chairman Mao put together.

Had the right roads been taken, today's world might have a population of 3 to 4 billion—a more peaceful, better fed, more educated, more biologically diverse, and more sustainable world. Somewhere between 1950 and 2050, for the first time in literally billions of years, one species—our own—has (or will) exceed the capacity of the biosphere to sustain our lifestyle. We will be doing irreversible damage to a fragile planet and stealing resources from our children and grandchildren.

Augustine, the Vatican, Jesse Helms, Pope Paul and all who try to keep women shackled to involuntary reproduction, you have more to answer for than your blinkered, biased minds could have possibly envisaged.

Malcolm Potts, MB, BChir, PhD, FRCOG, is a Cambridge (England)-trained obstetrician and biologist. He now holds the Bixby Chair of Population and Family Planning at the University of California, Berkeley. He obtained a double first in Natural Sciences at Cambridge and did his clinical training at University College London. He was elected a Fellow of Sidney Sussex College in 1964 where he taught medicine and conducted basic research on the implantation stages of pregnancy in mammals. He was the medical spokesperson on radio and TV for the reform of the British abortion law in 1966.

Dr. Potts has been working internationally since 1968, when he became the first medical director of International Planned Parenthood Federation. In this capacity he wrote what was then the standard Textbook of Contraceptive Practice, and many protocols and training manuals for the IPPF and WHO. He conceptualized and coined the widely used phrase Community Based Distribution (CBD), to enable teachers and other people at the village level to perform a variety of task that were commonly considered medical, including the distribution of family planning. In 1972, he published the first description of vacuum aspiration abortion. He was on the founding boards of Ipas, Marie Stopes International, Population Services International (where he still serves), and Family Health International. He was appointed President and CEO of FHI in 1978, where he initiated the first beyond-urban research on maternal mortality, was responsible for collaborative research work in family planning, lactation amenorrhea, contraceptive development, and HIV prevention in 40 countries. He had executive responsibility for training in research design and implementation and scientific writing. He also set up ethical committees in a number of countries.

In 1992, Dr. Potts was selected as the first person to fill a Bixby Endowed Chair in the University of California system. In 2008 he created at U.C. Berkeley the Bixby Center for Population, Health and Sustainability.

Professor Potts has worked in over 80 resource-constrained countries. In the past five years his work has taken him to China, Tanzania, Nigeria, Kenya, Ethiopia, Egypt, Uganda, Afghanistan, Pakistan, India, Iran, Thailand, Bangladesh and Sri Lanka, with an emphasis on safe motherhood, south-south supply of essential drugs, and family planning. He is the principal investigator in a NIH-Fogarty supported program in northern Nigeria.

Professor Potts has written 11 books and published over 350 papers and articles. His more recent books include *Queen Victoria's Gene*, tracking the haemophelia gene in the British royal family; and *Ever Since Adam and Eve: The Evolution of Human Sexuality.*

Dr. Potts newest book came out in 2009, titled *Sex and War: How Biology Explains Warfare and Terrorism and Offers a Path to a Safer World.* He has been a frontline witness to conflict around the world. He has worked with governments, aid organizations, and women who have been raped and brutalized in the course of war. In combining personal experience with scientific findings in genetics and anthropology, he explains war's pivotal position in the human experience and how men in particular evolved under conditions that favored gang behavior, rape and organized aggression. Dr. Potts charts a course for making warfare less frequent and less brutal, the power of ideas put into practice.

The Pioneers
by Donald A. Collins

I recall some of the pioneers on whose shoulders our leaders should be standing but sadly are not! It is too bad current world leaders have forgotten the ardor of their betters, who in the 1960's and early 70's understood population issues, and were committed to solving core problems, rather than tinkering at the edges. Now it is too late to do so without much pain.

My advice is simple. Insure the human rights of all women by providing free of charge all reproductive services, as only by so doing can the deadly population bulge be slowed and brought into balance with the rest of nature so that human life on our planet can be sustained.

That advice comes as the result of a long career in family planning. In September 1965, at age 34, armed only with a liberal arts BA and an MBA, I was hired as a program officer by a foundation group in Pittsburgh, Pa, whose major interests included family planning, then a rather arcane subject which had few devotees or non-profit entities to do the work. India's population was under 500 million, the United States under 200 million, total world population was 3.3 billion vs only 2 billion people in the world when I was born in 1931.

Now world humans number over 7 billion en route to a projected 9 or 11 billion by 2100, while most world leaders still whine about the need for endless growth, which a few prescient observers have dubbed 'the behavior of cancer cells'. Defining "growth" has often been focused on JOBS, which the Sunday September 8, 2013 CBS *60 Minutes* segment clearly showed are not coming back in any great numbers to the U.S. after this recession, due to automation and cheaper labor elsewhere.

Ignoring population growth by U.S. and other world leaders was not always so, as the late Lawrence Lader opined in his classic 1971 book, *Breeding Ourselves to Death*. The book recounted a history of strong support from a bipartisan cross-section of Americans including a past and present American President, both convinced about the dangers of world population expansion beginning to burgeon wildly.

One of my principal bosses at my new 1965 job was an immensely rich, retiringly shy, but forcefully committed population/family planning partisan named Cordelia Scaife May, whose Mellon forebearers had left her one of America's wealthiest women. (Her wonderful charitable legacy was briefly covered in a July 25, 2013 LA Times article.) At her urging, the several charitable entities that she influenced sought ways to extend family planning services to all women in the U.S. and around the world. There were few non-profit foundations then actively involved in providing such services, although the International Planned Parenthood Federation's network of affiliates around the world included its U.S. affiliate Planned Parenthood Federation of America (PPFA). PPFA was then, as now, certainly the leading U.S. family planning service provider. PPFA had been founded by Margaret Sanger. Cordelia May, "Cordy" as she was known, had come to know Sanger through her mother and was greatly influenced by her.

Early in my tenure at being a philantropoid (vs being a philanthropist—one who actually has the money), my workaday boss, the chief foundation manager, showed me a funny plastic item. "Do you know what that is?" I didn't. "It's an inter-uterine device and you are going on the board of National Planned Parenthood". Oops, talk about a naif in training.

I spent the next seven years on that PPFA board, meeting a who's who of family planning pioneers of that era: Bill Draper Sr, Hugh Moore, Alan and Leonore Guttmacher, Fred Jaffe, Bernie Barrelson, Frank Notestein, Paul Todd, Stewart Mott, Rei Ravenholt, Malcolm Potts, Julia Henderson, Al Moran, Bud Harkavy, Elton Kessel, Tim Black, Phil Harvey, George Denniston, and many more far too little lauded people who came forward to help facilitate more reproductive services for all women. There are so many more whose advice and counsel were so generously and freely given to me that I apologize for not having the space to bless them all.

My first international family planning meeting in Santiago, Chile in 1966, convened by International Planned Parenthood, was attended by many of those named above, plus Dr. M. C. Chang, the co-developer with Gregory Pincus, of the famous birth control pill approved by the FDA in 1960. I asked Dr. Chang how did they know how much progesterone to put in their initial Pill, to which he replied, "We really didn't know exactly". Over the years, of course, doses were minimized and one could rightly argue that The Pill was by far the most important invention of the last century. When combined with other methods, it brings the world the potential to be the greatest solution possible to save our plundered planet.

A major place to invest charitable funds for family planning in those early years was the Population Counsel (PC), founded in 1952 by John D. Rockefeller III. PC was willing, but only with approval from a sovereign government, to fund contraceptive services in foreign countries. A major initial effort in IUD distribution in Taiwan got Cordy's approval and had proved very successful by the time I joined the Pittsburgh charitable staff.

Cordy subsequently toured Asia with PC President Frank Notestein, gaining first-hand knowledge of conditions on the ground, which helped inspire later more daring philanthropy. To her, the numerous weighty formal studies of population trends and methods had by then already proved the obvious: the real work was to provide specific birth control services as rapidly and widely as possible. Those services included providing safe, early if possible, abortions. Of course abortions were not available in the U.S. on demand until the historic *Roe v Wade* Supreme Court decision of January 23, 1973. We now know that this ruling triggered a full-scale attack on family planning led by the Roman Catholic Church, which has proved to be one of the most dangerous and effective attacks on basic human rights mounted in the 20th Century, and continuing today.

Well before the passage of *Roe v Wade*, there were states that could do abortions and I was dispatched to find abortion funding service opportunities, which were provided by all too few around the nation. When New York State passed its abortion on demand law in July, 1971, the CEO of NYC's PPFA affiliate, Alfred Moran, took up the cudgel and quickly established substantial services, again aided substantially with Cordy's money. Her funds also created a revolving loan fund at PPFA to set up abortion clinics at any PP affiliate which wished to do so.

My own extensive tour of South America with an official of IPPF-Western Hemisphere in the late 1960's was where I observed women in hospital wards dead from septic abortions. This sealed my fervent commitment to fostering safe services.

In 1971, Dr. Ravenholt, then the head of the U.S. government Office of Population (1965 to 1979) asked me if I could get my trustees to grant $50,000 to start an early abortion non-governmental organization (NGO) to work overseas. He hoped once begun he could get sustaining support from USAID. Senator Helm's amendment in 1973 stopped that source of money in its tracks. However, International Pregnancy Advisory Services, now called IPAS, was already underway with an office and small staff. I got elected Chairman and President only because I was connected to its startup money.

Fortunately, my boss, Cordy, continued to support this fledgling startup and over time gave IPAS over $1.5 million ($12 million in today's dollars). Without her resolve, IPAS would likely not be here today. It took my chief fund-raising colleague on the IPAS board, Dr. Leonard Laufe, a distinguished Pittsburgh OB/GYN, and I many years to gain enough additional support from brave donors to bring IPAS forward. Celebrating 40 years of effective training and service this year, IPAS now enjoys major support from a growing number of large private donors, but still the Helms Amendment keeps our government from being involved.

Another hugely successful abortion services provider, UK headquartered Marie Stopes International, was started by Dr. Tim Black and Philip Harvey in the mid 1970's. They also started Population Services International (PSI) another major family planning commodity provider funded early by my then employer.

As former USAID Administrator, Duff Gillespie, writes, "As director of USAID's Office of Population from 1965 to 1979, Dr. Reimert T. Ravenholt created a family planning juggernaut that still provokes both praise and disdain. Ravenholt was a remarkable leader, full of perplexing contradictions. He dazzled people with his brilliance one moment and shocked them with his myopic ethnocentrism the next. He could be strategically wise and tactically reckless. Ravenholt's controversial reputation masks his many contributions, which are still evident 20 years after he was forced from his leadership of USAID's population program."

One of Dr. Ravenholt's many creations was International Fertility Research Programme (IFRP), under the founding leadership of Elton Kessel, MD, MPH, in 1971, again with critical startup money from Cordy's trusts which allowed IFRP to become independent of the University of North Carolina where it originally functioned, much to the delight of Senator Jesse Helms who sought its departure. Again, as a possible funding representative, I was asked to join its initial board where I served until about 2004. Now known as FHI360 (formerly Family Health International or FHI) and operating with a wide development and family planning mandate, its staff numbers thousands and its total yearly revenues approach $800 million.

FHI's second President, Dr. D. Malcolm Potts, now Bixby Professor of Population and Family Planning at UC Berkeley, sent a proposal in 1985 to USAID and obtained its first major grants to curb the HIV/AIDS epidemic. Then, a few years ago, at UC Berkeley, along with his wife, Dr. Martha Campbell, Potts helped found Venture Strategies, which assists a growing number of developing nations to better cope with the fatalities to mothers associated with postpartum bleeding.

While in Pittsburgh, my charitable fund employers approved my recommendations for start-up funding for a number of other family planning entities including Population Services International, Guttmacher Institute, Population Institute, Religious Coalition for Reproductive Choice, Population Dynamics, and others who have gone on to make the family planning movement stronger and more widely effective.

At present, as founder and President of International Services Assistance Fund, I and my colleagues, which include Dr. Jack Lippes, Dr. Stephen Mumford and Dr. Elton Kessel, are seeking FDA approval to market a inexpensive permanent method of female contraception, known as QS (invented by distinguished Chilean MD, Dr. Jaime Zipper) using a now well established standard protocol. QS has been provided by over 1,900 practitioners in over 50 countries to over 175,000 women, some for over 30 years, with no reports of deaths or major complications.

Thus, as noted initially, my message to world leaders is very simple. Leaders! You must use your full influence to work to insure basic human rights for all the world's women. Those rights must include the absolute right to decide when and under what circumstances they choose to bear children. That right can only be achieved with the full availability of safe, free or very inexpensive, modern contraception, including abortion. With over 40 million abortions occurring yearly world wide, we can only assume that contraceptive failure will continue. Thus, providing safe, preferably early—on demand if needed—services must accompany any family planning program to be effective and in keeping with offering women their full human rights.

As we now know, unless such programs are urgently initiated, a sustainable and humane habitation of our planet will continue to deteriorate. Failing to provide family planning, we can with certainty expect the growing disruptions presently visited on so many countries to spread globally as the 21st Century unfolds. Constant articles about various human disasters in the press seem to make no impression. And so the future remains cloudy.

Donald A. Collins is a former U.S. Navy officer, banker and venture capitalist. He is now a free-lance writer living in Washington, DC. He spent over 40 years working for women's reproductive health as a board member and/or officer of numerous family planning organizations including Planned Parenthood Federation of America, Guttmacher Institute, Family Health International and IPAS .

Mr. Collins holds a BA from Yale University and an MBA from New York University. He served with the U.S. Navy from 1953 to 1956. Subsequent to the U.S. Navy, Collins entered the commercial banking business in NYC. Thereafter, he became CEO of a Pittsburgh-based small business investment company. In 1965, he became Chief Administrative Officer of a Pittsburgh charitable foundation, which focused on community development, plus serving as a program officer of two other charitable entities with broad domestic and international mandates. In this connection, for 10 years, Collins helped develop a number of charitable programs concerned with forming public policy and service-based actions in the population and environment fields, including serving on the original boards of Advocates for Youth (then Center for Population Options), Alan Guttmacher Institute, International Projects Assistance Services, Family Health International (now FHI360) and others.

In 1976, Collins moved west and formed his own firms, Donald A. Collins Associates and International Services Assistance Fund, through which he engages in consulting activities for both for-profit and non-profit entities. His clients include several private foundations, for-profit corporations as well as individuals who seek advice on policy, program, organizational and operational management.

His primary interests remain in the fields of family planning and immigration reform. As an active volunteer, he encourages the use of a major new method of non-surgical female sterilization known as quinacrine sterilization (QS) for which he seeks advocates and funders. The same is true for immigration reform where he served for years on the board of the Federation for American Immigration Reform (FAIR), now serving as Co-Chair of its National Advisory Board.

Don also contributes OP ED pieces and letters to editors on these issues to newspapers, journals and blog sites. His latest book is *From the Dissident Left: A Collection of Essays 2004-2013*. It is available through Amazon.com

His 1976 marriage to Joan F. Kraus Collins ended with her death in 1993.

In November 1994 he married Sarah Gamble Epstein (the daughter of Dr. Clarence Gamble who founded Pathfinder International). Together they have been pursuing the task of seeking FDA approval for QS and other family planning work. They are still indefatigable travellers. Their most recent trip was to Patagonia and to the Iguassu Falls, seeing 275 separate waterfalls.

What is Required
by David Poindexter

In 1970, at the time he received the Nobel Peace Prize, Dr. Norman Borlaug declared, " I may have bought humankind an extra 35 or 40 years with my *Green Revolution,* but if we do not move now to destroy the monster of population growth we shall destroy our civilization and our species." Now, more than four decades on, it is apparent that Dr. Borlaug's words were solidly on target.

Because of Borlaug's leadership, South Asia saw a five-fold increase in cereal grain production in only 25 years, a record never matched in Europe or North America. For a few decades it ended the time of famines in Asia. Sadly, at the same time, there was no adequate effort to destroy the monster of population growth by the South Asian nations, or for that matter elsewhere on our planet.

In 1994, the UN International Conference on Population and Development in Cairo spelled out the funding requirements necessary to increase programs sufficiently to make the destruction of the monster of population growth possible. The level of response of the member nations that signed the Cairo Declaration during the next two decades has fallen so far short of basic requirements as to permit the "monster" to roam freely. Indeed during the four past decades since Dr. Borlaug focused our attention on this issue, the total number of humans on Earth has doubled from fewer than 4 billion to slightly under 8 billion this year.

If humankind is to slip out of the monster's stranglehold, what is required at this late date is

- A much more widespread recognition of the dire fate that awaits Earth's people if this threat remains on the back burner of global priorities.
- A clear demographic diagnosis of the nature of the monster. Currently, we hear a great deal about unmet need, when the reality points to inadequate demand. Studies have shown that in general there are family planning services available. They are not being adequately utilized because of male opposition, cultural traditions and religious opposition, fears of contraceptive side effects, and other readily recognizable factors such as the fear of the impact of aging populations, and fatalism both at the micro level (God sends the children) and the macro level, "population growth will solve itself. We have but to wait for it to level off."
- The mobilization planetwide of resources to bring into play the methods which work, beginning with gender equity and the involvement of the women of the planet.

In point of fact, the green revolution required much irrigation. Now with climate change and with the depletion of underground aquifers, we face a situation where drought will be a spreading reality. What will have to be done to defeat the "monster" must be accomplished as we move once again into a time of famines, no longer a disaster of the distant past. It is a specter looming over humankind's future. And there is a catalog of related ills stalking us, some of which doubtless are pointed out by other "elders" in this book. The basis of these ills is grounded in human behavior or perhaps more accurately, misbehavior.

In the mid 20th century, the Hugh Moore Fund sponsored a slogan contest. The one that won declared, "Whatever your cause, it's a lost cause if we don't stop population growth."

Toynbee's *Study of History* told us that Societies progress when there is a creative minority in leadership and the mass public follows through a process of "mimesis". What we do know, because of the research and findings of Professor Albert Bandura of Stanford University, is that behavior is the result of role modeling. It may be that the central effort of our time should be to mobilize Toynbee's creative minority so as to provide the requisite body of role models.

❖

David O. Poindexter is a native of the state of Oregon. He earned his bachelor's degree at Willamette University. He earned two advanced degrees, in theology and psychology at Boston University.

Poindexter has four decades of experience in designing and implementing reproductive health communications programs in developing countries, using the entertainment-education methodology created by Miguel Sabido. He has done this work as Director of the Communications Center of the Population Institute, founder and President of Population Communications International, and most recently as a program consultant and Honorary Chair for Population Media Center.

David started his career in the Methodist Church. From 1965 to 1969 he spent time with the Broadcasting and Film Commission of the National Council of Churches based in New York City where he became acquainted with the programs and personnel of the broadcast networks as well as the film industry. In 1969, Rodney Shaw, a respected colleague who was founding the Population Institute and who saw the need to use mass media, invited him to direct the Population Communication Center—which led to a lifetime of work promoting family planning and reproductive health in the U.S. and worldwide.

During the decade of the 1970s, David Poindexter was successful in mobilizing the producers and creators of numerous prime-time U.S. television shows, such as *Maude, All in the Family*, and *The Mary Tyler Moore Show*, to incorporate discussions of family size and sexual stereotyping into the context of these shows.

He then applied the "Sabido method" of social content *telenovela* to countries in Asia, Africa and Latin America, taking into account each country's widely varied culture, needs and reality. His family planning and empowerment of women soap operas are legendary in places such as Brazil and Tanzania.

David Poindexter was awarded the Everett M. Rogers Award for Achievement in Entertainment-Education in 2008. "David, like no other, saw the potential of the entertainment-education strategy early. Then, over the next four decades, he worked tirelessly around the globe to enlist the political will and resources to make it happen," says University of Texas communication professor Arvind Singhal, the 2005 recipient of the Rogers Award.

He is the author of the book *Out of the Darkness of Centuries*, the story of his odyssey to discover the use of mass media for human betterment.

Do What Your Mother Told You
by William N. Ryerson

As a global leader, you have, for too long, ignored the advice your mother gave you when you were growing up. It's time for you to reform your behavior. Let me remind you what she said.

Do Your Homework

You cheated yourself and the rest of us by skipping math and science courses in favor of political science and economics. While you were attending meetings of the young political leaders club, you missed entirely the teachings of ecologists, who were talking about carrying capacity and species extinction, population biology, and the power of the exponential function. But it's not too late.

You can take remedial education. Plenty of scientists would gladly provide free, after-school classes to help you understand what is driving the growing threat of our planet becoming uninhabitable because of the excessive demands of humanity on nature's services.

And don't forget to read the writings of social scientists like Harvard psychologist Solomon Asch and Stanford psychologist Albert Bandura, as well as brain scientist Paul MacLean, so you can understand what is causing collective human behavior to lead us toward global catastrophe and what can be done about it.

Also, subscribe to Population Media Center's email news service so you continue to learn what is truly important in world news.

Treat Others the Way You Would Want Them to Treat You

You hold office despite not having received a single vote from the millions of species that inhabit the Earth along with humans. But it's time for your human rights commissioner and your justice minister to recognize that each of these species has an equal right to exist. This means all species have an equal claim to the land and natural resources as humans. Stop looking the other way when your friends order shark fin soup or give ivory carvings as gifts. Or when your developer friends tear down forests to build houses and shopping malls. Human self-centeredness and your silence are driving thousands of species toward extinction. You may not have learned this in economics class, but the intricate web of life that has evolved over the last four billion years is all that is keeping you and your family and friends alive. Without the other species, we're toast.

Might Does Not Make Right

The ability of the wealthy classes to live opulent lifestyles does not make such consumption acceptable. Indeed, over-consumption is a major factor in many of the trends that threaten the most vulnerable people—and other species—including climate disruption, ocean acidification, toxification of the planetary environment, soil degradation, and much more.

Clean Your Room

You and your cohorts have made a real mess of our living quarters, and it's time you took responsibility for cleaning it up. In the pursuit of profits or narrow self-interest, you have allowed—and even supported—industrial and military forces to wreak havoc on the planet. Much of this activity has been in the search for non-renewable resources. Indeed, much of the human economic enterprise is not sustainable and will lead to ecological collapse if we don't change direction. Plan for a future 100 percent dependent on renewable resources. Ask your ministers of planning and environment to make an honest assessment of natural resource sufficiency, and then report to your people what this means in terms of lifestyle options and number of people that can be supported at any given level of economic activity. Then plan how to get your country's population to a level that can be sustained at the lifestyle the country chooses to pursue. It's not hard and can be done within a human rights framework, but get going on it now, or you will be badly tripped up when the rapidly depleting nonrenewables run out.

Don't Put Off Until Tomorrow What You Can Do Today

Postponing action until after the next election or until you are out of office is not acceptable and is a major reason we are in such a pickle. Go back to the dictionary and read the definition of "leadership," and then start acting like a leader. If you do, you will be honored by future generations. If you shirk your responsibility, you will be rightfully scorned.

Eat Your Vegetables

The growing appetite for meat worldwide is a major contributor to rising greenhouse gasses, loss of biodiversity, poor health, and starvation. In your own life, and in your policies, favor vegetarian diets, and shun excessive meat consumption. Stop subsidizing the beef industry, and impose steep taxes on all harmful food products.

Don't Go Along With the Crowd

In the 1950s, Harvard psychologist Solomon Asch showed that, for most people, fitting in is more important than telling the truth. Being popular is a major motivator for most politicians. Your instincts—and your pollsters—let you know what topics are too touchy to mention—even if they are vitally important.

Take the population issue. When's the last time you instructed your climate czar to examine the impact of adding 83 million people per year to the world's population? Even though most of this growth is occurring in countries with the lowest per capita greenhouse gas emissions, from now to 2050, the median projected growth will be roughly the climate equivalent of adding two United States to the planet. Also, thinking that the poor don't matter when it comes to climate change is to take the position that the poor are virtuous only as long as they remain poor.

Indeed, growing numbers of people—all aspiring to live comfortable lives—is driving unemployment, poverty, poor health, loss of habitat of other species, and conflicts over resources, and is a major unacknowledged threat to global habitability.

Honesty is the Best Policy

Your constituents are not hoping you'll take the easy way out and opt for the status quo. On the population issue, for instance, look at the data on the reasons people give for non-use of contraception. It is clear from Demographic and Health Surveys that the major barriers are misinformation about safety and efficacy, male opposition, religious opposition, and fatalism. Misinformation campaigns have falsely convinced many people that contraceptives lead to such health effects as cancer or permanent sterility. Many counselors fail to address real side effects with their clients. The 25,000 girls a day who are put into marriages before they are adults do not realize they have human rights, since they are being brought up by their husbands and can only take orders from them. Many other women are intimidated through violence and deprivation. Keeping all girls in school—including using public funds to provide them with sanitary napkins and washrooms so they don't stay home one week out of every four—will do far more for the future of most countries than any amount spent on armaments.

Increasing access to contraceptive services is necessary, but that is not the proximate barrier for most of the women who do not want to be pregnant but are not using a method of family planning. Large desired family size is still an important driver of high fertility rates in some countries, like Nigeria. Communications—especially use of entertainment media to model positive reproductive health behaviors—are vitally important to overcoming the cultural and informational barriers to contraceptive use and small family norms.

You need to lead the global community toward shrinking humanity's footprint. This means celebrating population shrinkage where it occurs and promoting sub-replacement fertility worldwide. Don't even think of using public funds to subsidize increasing the birth rate. Celebrate aging, and raise retirement ages to reflect the greater longevity achieved in the last century.

Don't Pick a Fight You Can't Win

If you have paid attention, you have learned that fighting Mother Nature is a losing proposition. We can win the battle for global sustainability, but only if you make it a priority.

When you think about it, sustainability is the ultimate environmental issue, the ultimate health issue, and the ultimate human rights issue. Please devote the rest of your career to leading us toward a sustainable future.

❖

William N. Ryerson is Founder and President of Population Media Center (www.populationmedia.org) an organization that strives to improve the health and wellbeing of people around the world through the use of entertainment-education strategies. He also serves as Chair and CEO of The Population Institute in Washington, DC (www. populationinstitute.org) which works in partnership with Population Media Center.

In developing countries, PMC creates long-running serialized dramas on radio and television, in which characters evolve into role models for the audience resulting in positive behavior change. The emphasis of the organization's work is to educate people about the benefits of small families, encourage the use of effective family planning methods, elevate women's status, prevent exploitation of children, and promote avoidance of HIV infection. To date, PMC has worked in over 50 countries.

Mr. Ryerson has 42 years of experience working in the field of reproductive health, including 25 years in adapting the Sabido methodology of social change communications to various cultural settings worldwide.

Ryerson received a B.A. in Biology (Magna Cum Laude) from Amherst College and an M.Phil. in Biology from Yale University (with specialization in Ecology and Evolution). His interest in, and understanding of, population issues started early; as a graduate student, he was Founder and first Chairperson of the Yale Chapter of Zero Population Growth (ZPG). He served as Director of the Population Institute's Youth and Student Division, Development Director of Planned Parenthood Southeastern Pennsylvania, Associate Director of Planned Parenthood of Northern New England and Executive Vice President of Population Communications International before founding Population Media Center in 1998.

Bill is listed in several editions of *Who's Who in the World*, *Who's Who in America* and *Who's Who in the East*. In 2006, he was awarded the Nafis Sadik Prize for Courage from the Rotarian Action Group on Population and Sustainable Development. Bill states, "I think population growth is one of the great root causes of poverty, unemployment, political instability, environmental destruction, energy shortages, species extinction, and other problems plaguing humankind."

A Moral Call to Action
by Linn Duvall Harwell

Three books inform my essay to world leaders: *Man Makes Himself*, a Sociology textbook; *The Time of Man*, transcendental words of priest-anthropologist, Teilhard de Chardin; and more recently, *Red Sky at Morning, Sailor Take Warning, Red Sky at Night, Sailor's Delight*, by author James Gustav Speth, retired Dean of Yale's School of Forestry and Environmental Studies.

It has been many years since I read *Man Makes Himself*, a book that gave me my best lesson in Sociology at the University of Connecticut. Every human has options, it suggests. Therefore, educated, compassionate people may be rewarded when they agree with Marcus Aurelius that "Man exists for the sake of one another; teach him, then or bear with him." I add, woman.

Teilhard de Chardin, through his enlightenment, encourages all of us to experience a transcending relationship when things go wrong. This relationship is more beneficial in accomplishing a noble purpose. The book was a challenge to me, and I absorbed his lessons. My wish is that all world leaders read it and internalize its message.

James Gustave Speth, author of *Red Sky*, brings the reader up to date with a future of expanding oceans due to climate change. He writes of the challenge of the wealth and danger the massive waters of our globe provide. Speth has encouraged expansion of environmental studies at Yale University. This is a great benefit to its students and future generations.

Through these books is woven the maleness of the human species.

Then came the voices of women who began to break the chains. They were cries of pain, indignation, resentment, anger, determination, cries for freedom of the femaleness of human society. Many of these female voices of reason resound in our time of man and woman. The late Margaret Mead, anthropologist, thrust her long pole to the Earth as she walked and talked to the leaders of the family planning movement. Hers was the challenge to look back at human origins to understand what humans do today.

These signs, road-marks of evolution, were seized by Betty Friedan, Eleanor Smeal, Sarah Weddington, each calling for recognition of the rights of women and for their contribution to human society. These names are but a sample of those who have demanded equality. Consider your own remembrances, adding other names of women who have provided benefits for the future of man and womankind.

As de Chardin and Mead looked backward to the social conduct of male and female, we are required to look forward to a trying, challenging future for the Seventh Generation, even to its very survival, solutions which avoid war and award diplomacy, respecting our capacity to reason. As the world careens toward 9 billion people and beyond, the survival of humanity may be difficult in the face of increasing crowding, climate disruption and nuclear proliferation.

These thoughts and emotional responses may lead to the sailor's delight in sexual engagement for which preventive protection offers a balanced benefit for both male and female: family stability and evolutionary advance supporting a moral call to action.

The big question is: "Are we there yet?" Not until we are all singing the same song—justice for that fifty percent (women and girls) who are half this nation's and this world's population.

Who holds some answers? Who holds ALL the answers? Were populationists to put it all together—challenging climate change, working for sustainability, survivability, equality—justice would prevail. Not one voice, but many voices!

Leaders of the world, invest in our future, not just with money. Money can't cut it. Hear the words of the late Herman Kahn, scientist: "Apocalyptic events pale to human loss of morale!" Look back in listening and learning—look forward in compassion and unity. Death by 1000 cuts—or life by 1000 condoms? Choice, that beautiful word, must be granted to both woman *and* man for a happier, healthier, more successful outcome.

Recalling the 1994 UN ICPD (United Nations International Conference on Population and Development) and words of Gro Harlem Brundtland, the woman who was Prime Minister of Norway at age 41: "We are gathered to answer a moral call to action. We are faced with the possibility of global bankruptcy. There is no single action that brings more immediate results than investing in the education of women. Morality becomes hypocrisy if it means accepting the misery of women and children worldwide. We must be responsible towards future generations. The Cairo Programme of Action must be successful for Earth's sake and for humanity's sake." This was Dr. Brundtland's greeting to us as she took the stage with Dr. Nafis Sadik, Madame Mubarak of Egypt, and Tipper Gore, wife of the U.S. Vice President.

Her words were a challenge to all world leaders in 1994, and they remain the challenge to each of us today.

Linn Duvall Harwell describes herself as a professional volunteer in the family planning movement, not an academician. Tragically, at a very young age she learned first-hand how a lack of family planning can destroy a family.

Her mother and father met on a riverboat in Pittsburgh, Pennsylvania; were married, she age 18, he 20, during WWI. They were poor. Babies were conceived; only 5 survived. Her mother, Clara, had a total of 8 pregnancies, the last ended in death by her own hand in an attempted illegal abortion. This was two weeks after Linn's sixth birthday.

Unable to care for five children, her father took them to Baltimore where they were divided between relatives and the Episcopal School for Girls. Within two weeks Linn had a birthday, lost her mother and father and all of her brothers and sisters. Many months later, her father moved the family to a farm where her sense of independence took root. For 6 years she attended a one-room country school. At age 16, she gathered up the courage to ask her grandmother why mother had died. Grandmother's first son died of diphtheria, second son of syphilis, and her only daughter, Linn's mother, from abortion. Her answer to Linn's question was "abortion." Linn claims right then and there her destiny was determined—her calling was to protect her life and the lives of women and girls everywhere.

Linn wed Howard Harwell on July 4, 1942 (during WWII). She recalls their first obligation was to seek contraception at Planned Parenthood. Her husband supported her work through 69 years of marriage. They moved to New Canaan, Connecticut, where at the First Presbyterian Church she was informed that contraception was against the law—the notorious Comstock Law prohibiting contraception and human sexuality education. Comstock was the nemesis of her hero, Margaret Sanger. She met Dr. Charles Lee Buxton, ob/gyn Yale Medical School and Estelle Griswold, CEO Planned Parenthood League of Connecticut. They provided her and other young mothers with contraceptive technology. She and her friends went into public housing to educate needy women. "If we were challenged, we had the right to free speech!" Linn recalls. It wasn't until June 1965 that the U.S. Supreme Court decided in favor of *Buxton & Griswold v Connecticut* for "birth control for married couples and protection for privacy of the bedroom." Linn was elated.

Moving to Philadelphia, she became a counselor at Philadelphia General Hospital and Bryn Mawr Hospital, two different cultures. She was elected to the board of Planned Parenthood. Through those contacts she was able to attend the first United Nations International Conference on Population, in Bucharest. That was an uplifting experience. The work back in the U.S. was not easy. She often became an object of criticism and verbal assault; nevertheless with two friends she formed what is now the third largest Planned Parenthood affiliate in Pennsylvania. In 1979, she created the Clara Bell Duvall Reproductive Freedom Project of the ACLU-PA in honor of her mother. In 1994, she again attended an international population conference, the UNICPD in Cairo.

Not content to work only for reproductive rights, Linn has served on the boards of various chapters of the League of Women Voters (LWV). In 1996, the LWV elected her to The National Women's Hall of Fame at Seneca Falls, New York.

In "retirement" in New Hampshire, she has remained very active in many New England sustainability groups, including the New England Coalition for a Sustainable Population. At age 90 Lynn's mental powers and energy remain undiminished, as she continues to advocate for the critical role women play in the protection of families, in reproductive education, in political advancement, and in the security of our beautiful blue planet.

What I Would Say to World Leaders
by Sarah G. Epstein

I have spent most of my life as a social worker in the field of family planning, so I am well aware of the advantages of contraception for families everywhere. Now my deepest concern is for the generation of my grandchildren and beyond. What kind of world are we leaving them? With world population today at more than seven billion and still growing, we are already robbing the future of fresh water, oil, adequate farmland, and the joy of untrammeled open spaces. We are already negotiating clogged roads, breathing smog-laden air, and losing somewhere near 100 species of animals and insects every day.

Each new disaster—flood, earthquake, fire—seems to kill and displace more people. And of course, the reason is that there are more people. If these ills are to be overcome, it will only be if there are far fewer people than are now here.

Therefore, our top priority should be to ensure that free contraception is available to everyone everywhere in all cities, towns, villages and rural areas of the world. Trained doctors, nurses and social workers, male and female, should make sure that all the world's inhabitants learn—through public meetings and discussions—about the health and economic benefits of small families with well-spaced children. Early marriage should be discouraged, and all children (especially girls) should be educated using a curriculum that includes health and sex education, food and nutrition, and ecology. And there should be an emphasis on human rights for all, in order to eliminate religious strictures, especially those that affect women.

I ask all world leaders to emphasize the need for a smaller population, brought about by educated people voluntarily choosing small families and a healthy lifestyle including good diet and exercise.

We live in a far different world than the one in which I grew up. I hope our external electronic brains and technological capabilities will help us reverse the effects of climate change and leave a better world. Only by reducing population to a level where the world can sustain itself can we hope to pass on a stable and safe world to our grandchildren. Endless population growth is suicidal!

Sarah Louise Gamble Epstein was born in 1925 in Philadelphia, Pennsylvania, to Sarah Bradley Gamble and Dr. Clarence James Gamble. She attended Germantown Friends School (Philadelphia), Milton Academy (Milton, MA), Wellesley College for two years, Oberlin College (Class of 1948) and Simmons School of Social Work. Since her father, Clarence Gamble, was an advisor to Margaret Sanger, she grew up believing all children were planned and wanted. When she realized this was not the case, she decided to work in the field of family planning. Her father was the founder of Pathfinder International, an organization that pioneered the provision of family planning services.

After a summer in Austria (1949) with the Experiment in International Living, she met Lionel Charles Epstein, a student at Harvard Law School and a participant in the Experiment program. They were married in 1951 and moved to Washington, DC, where they raised five children. She remained active with the Experiment and volunteered with Planned Parenthood, often counseling women in the maternity ward at the City Hospital. She was involved with Pathfinder International, and often traveled abroad to observe family planning programs at work.

She and Lionel were divorced in the early 1980s. She continued to travel and work in the family planning field. She met Donald Collins when he organized a group to go to Vietnam in 1993 to study a sterilization method called QS, which is a safe, sure, inexpensive and non-surgical permanent contraception for women. The QS procedure uses insertions of seven quinacrine tablets into the uterus. When they dissolve, they cause an inflammation inside the opening of the Fallopian tubes that results in a scar that seals the tubes closed. In Vietnam, they found that QS had been successfully used by thousands of women. Studies from around the world report no deaths or life threatening complications. However, after pressure from religious sources, the World Health Organization banned its use or further testing worldwide in 1993.

Shortly after returning from Vietnam, Sally married Don and they began work to have QS approved by the U.S. Food and Drug Administration. The FDA cancelled the Phase III trial for QS on the basis of an unscientific study that the FDA had designed and which overdosed the rats with enough quinacrine to cause cancer. Since then they have been stalled despite numerous meetings with the FDA.

However, they do not intend to give up. Too many women in the world are seeking just such a method so they can easily stop having more children when their families are complete.

Sally stays involved with many other international family planning programs. For example, she has helped Molly Melching, the founder of Tostan, to succeed with her educational program in Senegal where the villagers decided to abandon female genital cutting. The Tostan education program is spreading across Africa and now many more African villages are eliminating the practice.

My Population Pitch to 700,000 World Leaders
by Robert Gillespie

When I first started working in the family planning field, the world's human population was about 3 billion. In 2012 there were 7 billion and the population is headed to 11 billion before the turn of the century. Any country that does not have a plan of action to achieve population stabilization by lowering the birth rate, will stabilize population by an increase in the death rate. All world leaders need to be actively involved in achieving replacement-size families by improving the status of women, guaranteeing quality family planning services, and reinforcing a human rights approach to reproductive health and family planning.

Let's assume that there is one world leader for every 10,000 population who could take an action that would result in couples wanting and having two children. The 700,000 leaders would be given specific tasks that take into consideration their cultural, economic, social, political, religious, resource, historical and environmental backgrounds. These leaders comprise heads of government, cabinet members, governors-general, parliamentarians, the judiciary, presidents of universities, women's organizations, businesspersons, labor, religious denominations, youth groups, entertainment, sports and mass media plus the burgeoning world of cell phone and internet users. The actions required span from the cradle-to-the-grave and from dawn to dusk.

The path to the two-child family needs to focus on many

aspects of society: preventing maternal and child deaths, preventing coercive child marriages, giving young adults opportunities to prevent unintended and unwanted pregnancies, increasing the age at marriage to 20, birth spacing by 2 to 3 years, having a girl's birth celebrated as much as a boy's, creating empowerment by functional literacy, credit and cooperatives, having an alternative to child labor and to children supporting their aging parents.

What is often neglected is the power men acquire by having many children. In some cultures women want to have many children in order to prevent their husband from taking another wife and starting an additional family. Equally relevant is the lack of access to the methods that give sexually active couples the choice to choose when and how many children they want. There is a prevailing fear that the methods are not safe.

Successful services provide vasectomy, permanent female contraception, access to medical and surgical abortion, emergency contraception, levenorgesteral and copper IUDs, the ring, implants, injectibles and spacing methods such as oral contraceptives and condoms. You can read the results of a survey of contraceptive practices Population Communication conducted at teaching hospitals and training clinics in Bangladesh, Egypt, Guatemala, India, Nigeria and the Philippines on the website: www.populationcommunication. com.

Each country needs a blueprint for achieving population stabilization. Population Communication has contracted country specific reports for Bangladesh, Egypt, Ghana, the states of Bihar and Uttar Pradesh in India, Kenya, Mali, Nigeria, Pakistan, Philippines, Senegal, Uganda, Yemen, and Zimbabwe, which are available on our website. We have designed surveys specifically for religious leaders, traditional birth attendants, village leaders, school teachers, agricultural extension agents and trained health personnel in the public and private sectors.

The delivery of contraceptive services can be structured in the public and private sector by contracting with health providers based on their existing experience or qualifications after training, using fee-for-service payments. In countries without universal health care, full time family planning field workers are needed to visit every household twice a year. Mobile clinics, post-partum services, including using traditional birth attendants and social marketing, will increase access to contraceptive methods.

Fortunately there is a revived interest in family planning. On World Population Day, July 11, 2012, an initiative started by the Gates Foundation and DFID (the British government Department for International Development) established the goal of providing family planning services to 120 million women and girls with a pledge of an additional $2.6 billion. To read more, go to www.familyplanning2020. org. You can read the *18 FP2020 Questions and Challenges* on the Population Communication website.

In India 10 of the 18 states and union territories have TFRs (total fertility rates) of less than 2.2 and some states, such as Punjab, Tamil Nadu, Kerala, Andhra Pradesh, West Bengal, and Maharashtra all have TFRs below 2. There is nothing that needs to be done in Bihar, Uttar Pradesh, Madhya Pradesh and Rajasthan that hasn't been successfully accomplished in other regions of India. India continues to add 1.5 million new people every month even with declining birth rates because of the momentum built into the youthful age profile. Likewise, China with the One-Child Policy and a TFR of 1.5 still adds 560,000 new people every month.

The momentum built into the sub-Saharan Africa population is dramatic with 44% of the population below the age of 15. No matter how successful the family planning programs, the sub-Saharan populations will triple. To visualize this momentum we have prepared population projection charts with TFRs of 1, 2, and 3, current TFRs as reported by the Population Reference Bureau, and desired family size as reported in "Demographic and Health Surveys" on our website for the following countries: Bangladesh, Burkina Faso, Chad, Egypt, Ghana, India, Kenya, Liberia, Malawi, Nepal, Niger, Nigeria, Pakistan, Philippines, Sudan, Tanzania and Uganda.

Population Communication has initiated the *Statement on Population Stabilization** that has been signed by 75 heads of government. Each year national leaders receive the *Statement* and the population projections. An endowment is established to update the population stabilization reports and to include all countries with more than 10 million population and TFRs above 3. Vital statistic applications will be prepared for each of the priority countries that link population with CO_2 emissions, bio-diversity loss, deforestation, desertification, allocation of fresh water and the impact of the marine habitat. You can download two apps we have commissioned from the Apple store. The India Vital Statistics app has counters for population, births/ deaths, arable land lost, forest area, CO_2 emissions, species extinction,

Facing the Population Challenge

---

* Read the *Statement* in the "Documents" section of this book.

air pollution and desertification. The India Population Counter goes forward 50 years and backward 50 years. We have established an endowment to update the demographic and environmental statistics annually. We will soon have population projections and environment vital statistic applications for Nigeria and all the countries where we focus our activities.

I have had the privilege, pleasure and joy of designing family planning programs and population policies for 52 years. I will record this history in a book and include specific instructional materials on our website.

The 75 leaders who signed the *Statement on Population Stabilization* recognize all populations will eventually stabilize by lowering birth rates to replacement size families—or by increasing death rates. All economies must eventually adjust to a zero fossil fuel future. We live in an increasingly more precarious environment. With depleting water resources, deforestation, biodiversity loss, and increased carbon emissions, almost every environmental indicator is moving in the wrong direction. When we destroy our habitat, we destroy the capacity of future generations of children to survive. The problems are daunting but the opportunities plentiful.

Bob Gillespie is founder and President of Population Communication. When Population Communication was founded in 1977, the world's population was close to four billion. The more than seven billion people today are headed to eleven billion by the turn of the century. Population Communication's mission is to focus on communicating population messages to national leaders, and to develop innovative family planning programs. The organization is actively working on prescribing the actions to achieve replacement-size families by improving the status of women, guaranteeing quality family planning services, and reinforcing a human rights approach to reproductive health and family planning.

While visiting agricultural stations as a soil science student in Egypt in 1960, Bob Gillespie switched professions from helping farmers grow more food to helping sexually active couples prevent unwanted pregnancies. In 1962 and 63 he was a Pathfinder stationed in Hong Kong, where he developed community-based contraceptive services. From 1964 to 1976 he was the Population Council resident representative in Taiwan, Turkey, Iran, and Bangladesh, and advised the governments in India, Pakistan, the Philippines, and Indonesia on how to design national family planning programs and population stabilization policies. Then for three years he designed "beyond family planning" initiatives for Population Crisis Committee, now Population Action International.

Mr. Gillespie has established an endowment to communicate to national leaders worldwide the Statement on Population Stabilization. (Find the Statement in the "Documents" section at the end of this book.) Population projections for each country based on TFRs of 1, 2, and 3, the existing TFR and the desired family size are included in the mailing.

To reach more people in this electronic age, Bob has designed population projection apps available on the iPhone, including the 'India Population Counter'. His 'Indian Vital Signs' app shows population growth, the number of births and deaths as well as environmental vital signs, such as deforestation, desertification, bio-diversity loss, and carbon emissions. Soon fresh water and marine environment indicators will be added.

Bob stated: "During the 52 years that I have been designing family planning programs and population policies, the Earth has added 4 billion more people. Almost every environmental indicator is moving in the wrong direction. Not a happy picture for those who will be here in 2100."

Ending the Silence on Population
by Martha Campbell

There is so little attention in the media to population growth on our planet that one would think this subject is not important. Today there is a pervasive discomfort in talking about population, not only in the media but also among businesses, environmental organizations, universities and whole societies. Why?

In the 1980s and early 1990s a growing network of women in the U.S. and in developing countries began to increase attention to the many needs of women, based on multiple dimensions of empowerment. These needs included educating girls and women, providing health services, owning property rights, eliminating domestic violence, allowing for economic opportunities, and more. In 1992 the large Earth Summit took place over two weeks in Rio de Janeiro, Brazil. Its formal title was the United Nations Conference on Environment and Development. In the city's largest park tents were set up for the use of a variety of organizations. In the women's tent, which was the largest, many discussions took place, representing women from numerous countries, with an emphasis on the needs of women around the world.

Immediately after the Earth Summit the two years of formal preparations began for the upcoming United Nations International Conference on Population and Development (ICPD) in Cairo, Egypt in 1994. The ICPD's four formal UN preparatory meetings during those two years broadened and expanded on the concerns and needs for women. The formal document resulting from this two-year process, known as the Programme of Action, included attention to the importance of slowing population growth. In addition it called on eliminating the barriers that prevent women from having access to family planning. Extensive discussions led to highlighting at length the many kinds of changes needed for women in a wide variety of ways. It was a stunning document with laudable goals, and remains so today.

But something else happened during those two years. With generous donor support from a few foundations, a small core group of activists in the United States started teaching leaders of women's groups from around the world that population means coercion. They placed emphasis on the unfortunate sterilizations in India from 1975 to 1977, China's long held coercive contraceptive programs and forced abortions, and sad examples of sterilization in other countries.

The activists insisted that the family planning programs, such as those sponsored by the U.S. and a number of European countries' foreign aid agencies, were set up to encourage women to use contraceptives whether they wanted them or not. Many people were taught that all family planning before 1994 was coercive population control, while everything after Cairo was improving women's lives. The foreign aid family planning programs were disparagingly referred to as "population control", a term considered highly offensive today.

Oddly, and unfortunately, these same activists who focused on coercion in the past avoided mentioning the coercion of huge numbers of women in many countries who were, and still are today, forced to have pregnancies they did not want.

Tragically there were some truly unacceptable episodes of coercive family planning. No one denies India's unfortunate three years of sterilizations, the extended excesses in China, and other genuine examples of coercive sterilization. But the vast majority of family planning programs prior to 1994 were voluntary by far. These programs laid the foundation for the highly successful revolution in family planning in many countries ranging from Brazil to Thailand. The contraceptive freedom that women won enabled those nations to escape from poverty.

The Strategy of Silence Around Population

Following Cairo, using the terms "population" or "family planning" was considered politically incorrect. This was the beginning of a strange silence around population, which has lasted for decades. Within a short time the word "demographic" became a pejorative term—but interestingly, "demography" was not. I still occasionally hear in our university some signs of this fearful use of "demographic" in discussions around population. In the late 1990s, in many meetings in both European countries and the U.S., I observed widespread patterns of these kinds of thinking based on growing misinterpretations. These unfortunate beliefs grew into a kind of social indoctrination.

Out of the 1990s sad silence about population has come today's even broader silence around the population factor in today's changing world. Today's pervasive discomfort about this subject is still found in many women's advocacy groups, news media, businesses, environmental organizations, universities, and whole societies, as I have mentioned earlier.

At the time of the four UN preparatory conferences preceding the 1994 ICPD, the new term "reproductive health" was created, and it became an important element of the UN's formal and well written Program of Action, which defined ICPD. The term family planning still existed, but only quietly as it was subsumed under the term reproductive health. This was particularly interesting, because this broad term reproductive health has been attractive and useful, and continues to be so today.

An Unfortunate Decision

The late Joan Dunlop, a preliminary leader of the movement that created the silence, came to my office in California some months after Cairo, and said she knew family planning was important but it could wait until later years. Michelle Goldberg, in her dazzling 2009 book *The Means of Reproduction: Sex, Power, and the Future of the World*, quotes an interview with Dunlop: "We knew there were huge streams of money going into contraceptive development, and we wanted that money to go in a different direction." Dunlop had begun by saying half apologetically, "What we wanted to do was, rather, [not] simply throw the baby out with the bathwater; we wanted to redirect the money."

Unfortunately, the baby was indeed thrown out with the bath water.

The timing couldn't have been worse. Successful family planning programs that were dependent on foreign aid agencies for funds, and just beginning in countries like Kenya, stalled. Desperately needed programs in the least developed countries such as Niger never began. The delay in access to family planning over these 20 years has proved costly. It has helped facilitate a great deal of rapid population growth in impoverished parts of Africa. African demographer Alex Ezeh calculates that Kenya will have 12 million more people in the year 2050 than it would have had otherwise.

Take the example of the Sahel. This is the increasingly arid zone bordering the Sahara desert across Africa, where serious threats to food security are inevitable. In 1950 there were 30 million people in this region, and today there are 125 million. Family planning is barely available. In 2050 we can expect 320 million people. Climatologists estimate that the Sahel's extreme high temperatures, which today are uneven, will become the norm. The region's citizens who in 2050 will be in greater in number than the 316 million people who live in the U.S. today, could very well be watching their crops wither and their livestock die. The vast numbers of people likely to seek new livable places by migration will not always be welcome. The catastrophe ahead could be larger than AIDS.

The strategy of trying to switch family planning budgets to the broader needs of women was unfortunate in three ways. First, the foreign aid funds for family planning collapsed, due partly to AIDS expenditures, but in large part due to a shift of international donor agencies away from family planning.

Second, the strategy failed to help meet the multiple, genuine needs of women. In fact, the "huge streams of money going into contraceptive development" before ICPD never exceeded $15 million in any one year. By contrast, in order to overcome the inequities from which women suffered—and continue to suffer today—would have required not tens of millions of dollars, but tens of billions of dollars.

And third, the group who silenced the population subject and slowed down efforts to make family planning more widely available made it more difficult to lift millions of the world's most poor and vulnerable women out of poverty.

There is no need for the silence on population. It has been a costly error, set up by well-meaning people who genuinely believed they were helping women, while instead they were inadvertently doing harm.

Why Population Matters

In the least developing countries rapid population growth

presents insurmountable challenges to education, the environment, water, and food security. Demographer John May has pointed out that countries with an average family size of 4 or more, with the exception of a few oil-rich states, have not been able to develop. To describe this in another way, in countries where average size is high, many more children are born each year than the year before. In this situation their governments are not able to manage to keep pace with the rapidly growing needs for their education systems – the core of development.

What has this meant for women? It meant that when family planning foreign aid budgets were held back, women's opportunities for education were held back too, slowing efforts for women's empowerment. Education is important for women's advancement, but in many parts of poor countries being educated is too often not an option. The important changes that the well-meaning activists hoped and expected to achieve without attention to the population factor could not occur without enabling women to have, above all, the power to manage their childbearing through access to family planning, as they choose.

With thanks to the Gates Institute at Johns Hopkins University, three major conferences in Africa have brought family planning back onto the table. But partly because of the indoctrination during the years that followed the Cairo conference, there is still considerable silence about population, and we are lacking an explicit policy link between family planning and population.

The World Health Organization reports that in Africa every year some 6 million women submit to unsafe abortions. There is no doubt that women take this on in desperation, in the absence of any other options. Of these yearly 6 million women, 26,000 die from the dangerous and painful procedures, and many many more suffer from extended injuries, often to the end of their lives. They should never have to undergo this suffering.

Uniting Women's Rights with Population

Now it is time to look forward. We need to start by bringing together the importance of women's empowerment with attention to the damaging impacts of continued rapid population growth. And we need to remove the unjustified barriers that separate women from the information and means they need to separate sex from childbearing.

The medium variant projection of the UN Population Division for the world in 2100 is 10 billion people. If everyone in the world on average adds an average half a child more, then the population will skyrocket to 15.8 billion. By contrast, if everyone on average were to have a half a child fewer, then in 2100 there would be 6.2 billion people. If we continue to separate the population subject from the imperative to improve the status and health of women, there is risk that world population could drift well above 10 billion. Time is important, and yet we have been lacking any sense of urgency.

If we support a woman's right to decide how many children to have, and if we understand how rapid population growth undermines development, then we can produce a more logical, safer, and successful world. Keep in mind that a world of 6.2 billion would be better educated, better fed, and more peaceful than a world of 10 to 16 billion.

Clear and open knowledge about the population factor on this planet is critical to a rational and caring approach in this generation and the next.

I am the fourth of four daughters, and had the privilege of attending a women's college where our professors encouraged us to think boldly and independently. I was active in the two-week Earth Summit conference in 1992 at Rio, under a Rockefeller grant, and was present at Cairo, in addition to the preparatory meetings in the UN during the two years before it. For more than 5 years I had the privilege of directing the population program of a major foundation, where a central part of our program was reproductive rights.

One of Cairo's benefits was a rapid expansion of the number of women in many countries who were no longer tolerating a secondary position in societies where men, since time immemorial, had presumed they would always keep the lead. In the United States today it is a joy to see the growing rage among an increasing number of women fighting back against the extreme right wing politicians who seek constraints on women's reproductive lives.

It is time to unite the theme of women's rights with a concern and understanding of the population factor in the many challenges of today's world. Understanding together the importance of enabling women to manage their own childbearing, while recognizing the importance of population in the most constrained parts of the world, is critical for the benefit of today's women and their families, and for tomorrow's children.

❖

Martha Madison Campbell, PhD, is the founder and president of the nonprofit organization Venture Strategies for Health and Development (VSHD), and a Lecturer in the School of Public Health at the University of California, Berkeley. In 1994 she joined the David and Lucile Packard Foundation in Los Altos, California, directing the population program, which included reproductive rights.

VSHD (www.venturestrategies.org) achieved the first-ever regulatory approval of misoprostol tablets anywhere in the world for its use to control hemorrhage after childbirth (which is the largest cause of maternal deaths in nearly all countries). This was done at the request of three leading African obstetricians, and their first success was in Nigeria, in early 2006. Shortly afterward VSHD facilitated similar approvals in Tanzania, Ghana, Zambia, Bangladesh and Nepal. In 2008 VSHD created its partner organization Venture Strategies Innovations, which has continued this work for the benefit of women's health in many countries.

Martha has written and spoken on why there is silence and sensitivity around the subject of population growth. One of her recent articles, "The Impact of Freedom on Fertility Decline" was published with her husband Malcolm Potts and their colleague Angolan physician Ndola Prata at Berkeley. Another recent article titled "Do Economists Have Frequent Sex?" was written with Malcolm Potts for the *Population Press* (www.populationpress.org). Both of these papers have introduced a new paradigm challenging conventional theories about what causes birth rates to decline, and the importance of women's decisions about their own reproductive lives.

Earlier, Martha led the first comprehensive review of the broad range of barriers that in many countries make family planning extremely difficult for women to obtain, for both contraception and safe abortion. It is titled "Barriers to Fertility Regulation", published in 2006, and co-authored with Turkish physician Nuriye Nalan Sahin-Hodoglugil and Malcolm Potts. These publications can be found easily under bixby.berkeley.edu, then publications, under author, Campbell.

Martha serves on the boards of World Health Partners in New Delhi, the Margaret Pyke Trust in London, and the African Institute for Development Policy (AFIDEP) in Kenya. Her degrees are from Wellesley College and the University of Colorado.

II. Environment and Limits to Growth

Let's Save Civilization: A Letter to the President of the United States
by Lester R. Brown

Our early twenty-first century civilization is in trouble. We have created an economy that is destroying its natural support systems. None of the earlier civilizations whose archeological sites we now study survived the ongoing destruction of their environmental support systems. Nor will ours.

The Earth's forests are shrinking by 13 million acres per year. Soil erosion exceeds soil formation on one third of the world's cropland, slowly draining the land of its fertility. Half the world's people live in countries where water tables are falling, aquifers are being depleted, and irrigation wells are starting to go dry. The world's ever-growing numbers of cattle, sheep, and goats are converting vast stretches of grassland into desert, helping create huge new dust bowls. Four fifths of oceanic fisheries are being fished at capacity or beyond. Many are headed for collapse. In system after system, demand is overshooting the sustainable yield.

Meanwhile, with our massive burning of fossil fuels, we are overloading the atmosphere with carbon dioxide (CO_2), pushing the Earth's temperature ever higher. This in turn generates more extreme climatic events, including crop-withering heat waves, more intense droughts, more severe floods, more destructive storms, and melting ice sheets. If the Greenland ice sheet were to melt, sea level would rise 23 feet.

Economists, including those who advise you, look at the future through a very different lens. Projections of economic growth, whether by the World Bank, Goldman Sachs, Deutsche Bank, or any of a hundred other leading financial institutions, typically show the global economy expanding by roughly 3 percent a year.

Economists make growth projections almost in the abstract. They do not ask questions like how much water will it take to double the world economy by 2034? What will happen to the Earth's climate if we continue to burn the massive quantities of fossil fuels assumed in these projections? How will a doubling of the world economy affect the demand for food?

Food: The Weak Link

When we look back at earlier civilizations, the ones whose archeological sites we now study, more often than not it was food shortages that led to their demise. For the Sumerians, it was rising salt levels in the soil that reduced wheat and barley yields until eventually the civilization collapsed. For the Mayans, it was deforestation and soil erosion that set the stage for their downfall. Although I had long rejected the idea that food could be the weak link in our modern civilization, I now not only think it could be, but that it is.

On the demand side of the food equation, the consumption of grain is growing faster than ever before. Each year, the world adds 80 million people. Tonight, there will be 219,000 people at the dinner table who were not there last night, many of them with empty plates. In addition to the relentless growth of population, some 3 billion people are moving up the food chain, consuming more grain-intensive livestock products.

Even as population growth and rising affluence claim more grain, we are also converting grain into fuel for cars on a massive scale. In 2010, 126 million tons of the 400-million-ton U.S. grain harvest went to ethanol fuel distilleries, up from 16 million tons in 2000. Cars are now competing with people for the world's grain supply. And with this capacity to, in effect, convert grain into oil, the price of grain is now tied to that of oil. If at some point supply disruption drives the price of oil to $150 per barrel, or even $200, the price of grain will follow it upward.

As a result of these three demand-driven trends—population growth, rising affluence, and the use of grain to fuel cars—the annual growth in world grain consumption, which totals roughly 2.2 billion tons per year, has climbed from 20 million tons per year a decade ago to 40 million tons per year in recent years.

Climate Change, Overpumping, and Overplowing

On the supply side of the equation, farmers are confronted with several challenging new trends that are making it more difficult to expand production. Agriculture as it exists today has evolved to maximize production within a climate system that, despite occasional blips along the way, has been remarkably stable over the last 11,000 years. Now, as climate changes, agriculture is more and more out of sync with it. The rule of thumb among crop ecologists is that for every 1 degree Celsius rise in temperature above the optimum during the growing season, we can expect a 10 percent decline in wheat, rice, and corn yields. As temperature goes up, yields come down.

Water shortages are also emerging as a major constraint on food production. Today, water tables are falling as a result of overpumping for irrigation in some 18 countries that contain over half the world's people. Overpumping artificially inflates production until the aquifer is depleted, whereupon pumping is necessarily reduced to the rate of recharge. These water-based food bubbles are starting to burst.

The largest water-based food bubbles are in India and China. World Bank data indicate that 175 million Indians are being fed by overpumping. I estimate that 130 million Chinese are being fed with grain produced by overpumping. Irrigation wells are going dry in both countries. The unsettling reality is that peak water may now be behind us.

Rising temperatures and falling water tables are not the only problems. Soil erosion, as a result of overplowing and land mismanagement, is undermining the productivity of one-third of the world's cropland. Satellite images show two vast dust bowls forming—one stretching across northwestern China and western Mongolia, and the other across central Africa. Each year some 1,400 square miles of land in northern China turn to desert. Civilization can survive the loss of its oil reserves, but it cannot survive the ongoing loss of its topsoil.

Failing States

If I were to pick three indicators that will tell us where we are headed, the first would be an economic indicator: grain prices. The second would be a social indicator: the number of hungry people in the world. And the third would be a political indicator: the number of failing states.

As environmental stresses mount and as food prices climb, we are seeing an increase in what we have come to call failing states, countries where governments can no longer provide personal security, food security, or basic social services such as education and health care. Among these are countries like Haiti, Somalia, Afghanistan, Yemen, North Korea, Pakistan, Zimbabwe, and many others. These failing states become centers of piracy (Somalia) or the source of 90 percent of the world's heroin (Afghanistan) or safe havens for terrorist groups such as al-Qaeda and the Taliban (Pakistan).

Failing states are an early symptom of a failing global civilization. The list of failing states grows longer with each passing year, raising a disturbing question, namely, how many failing states before our global civilization begins to unravel? We do not know the answer to that question, but we do know that climate change, population growth, water shortages, food shortages, and rising food prices are accelerating this process.

This situation is deteriorating fast. Since it is the destruction of the economy's natural supports and disruption of the climate system that are driving the world toward the edge, these are the trends that must be reversed. Doing so requires extraordinarily demanding measures, a fast shift away from business as usual to what we at the Earth Policy Institute call 'Plan B'.

We need an economy for the twenty-first century, one that is in sync with the Earth and its natural support systems, not one that is destroying them. The fossil fuel-based, automobile-centered, throwaway economy that evolved in western industrial societies is no longer a viable model—not for the countries that shaped it nor for those that are emulating them. In short, we need to build a new economy, one powered with carbon-free sources of energy—wind, solar, and geothermal—one that has a diversified transport system and that reuses and recycles everything.

Turning to Plan B

Business as usual is no longer a viable option. The alternative, Plan B, can move us onto a path of sustainable progress, but it will take a massive mobilization—at wartime speed. This plan, or something similar to it, is our only hope.

Plan B has four components: a wartime-like mobilization to cut global carbon emissions 80 percent by 2020; the stabilization of world population at no more than 8 billion by 2040; the eradication of poverty; and the restoration of forests, grasslands, soils, aquifers, and fisheries.

Carbon emissions can be cut by systematically raising world energy efficiency, by electrifying transport systems, and by shifting from burning fossil fuels to tapping the Earth's natural wealth of wind, solar, and geothermal energy. The transition from fossil fuels to renewable sources of energy can be driven primarily by tax restructuring by steadily lowering income taxes and offsetting this with a rise in the tax on carbon.

Two of the components of Plan B—stabilizing population and eradicating poverty—go hand in hand, reinforcing each other. This involves ensuring at least a primary school education for all children—girls as well as boys. It also means providing rudimentary village-level health care, including importantly childhood immunization against infectious disease, so that parents can be more confident that their children will survive to adulthood. And women everywhere need access to reproductive health care and family planning services.

The fourth component, restoring the Earth's natural systems and resources, involves, for example, a worldwide effort to stabilize soils, an effort similar to that adopted by the United States during the Dust Bowl era of the 1930s. It also includes launching a worldwide effort to raise water productivity. This could be patterned after the highly successful international effort launched in the early 1960s that tripled world grainland productivity.

The Earth Policy Institute estimates that stabilizing population, eradicating poverty, and restoring the economy's natural support systems would take less than $200 billion of additional expenditures a year—less than one third of the U.S. military budget and a mere one eighth of the world military budget. In effect, the Plan B budget encompassing the measures needed to prevent civilizational collapse is the new security budget.

Creating an Honest Market

Moving onto the Plan B path, one that will sustain civilization, requires two policy initiatives: creating an honest market and updating our definition of security. The great weakness of our early 21st century global economy is that the market no longer tells the truth. Market prices include direct costs, but not indirect ones, which are often far larger.

Creating an honest market means restructuring taxes, lowering the tax on income and raising the tax on carbon so that the market price for fossil fuels reflects their true costs. Simply put this means lowering income taxes and offsetting this with a rise in the carbon tax. If we can create an honest market, then investments in efficiency will climb rapidly and new investments in energy production will shift from fossil fuels to renewable sources of energy. If we can get the prices right, the market will take care of the rest.

We are all economic decisionmakers, whether as corporate planners, government policymakers, investment bankers, or consumers. And we rely on the market for price signals to guide our behavior. But if the market gives us bad information, we make bad decisions, and that is exactly what we are doing.

Redefining Security

The second policy initiative is redefining security. We have inherited a definition of security from the last century, one that was dominated by two world wars and a cold war. Armed aggression may once have been a major threat to security. It no longer is. No one is going to attack the United States.

If we list the threats to our security in the 21st century, they would include climate change, continuing population growth, spreading water shortages, rising food prices, and a growing number of failing states. On my list, armed aggression does not make the top five on the list of today's threats to security.

Redefining security does not just mean redefining it only in conceptual terms, but also in fiscal terms. If we ask ourselves where do we get the financing for Plan B, it is clear that it comes from the reallocation of military budgets, a product of redefining security. The $200 billion of additional expenditures per year to implement Plan B is less than a third of the U.S. military budget and only one eighth of global military expenditures. We cannot say we don't have the resources. We do.

Douglas Alexander, former U.K. Secretary of State for International Development, put it well in 2007: "In the 20th century a country's might was too often measured in what they could destroy. In the 21st century strength should be measured by what we can build together."

Time: Our Scarcest Resource

Time is our scarcest resource. Nature determines the natural tipping point. Nature decides when the melting of the Greenland ice sheet becomes irreversible. Nature is the timekeeper, but we cannot see the clock.

Today we are in a race between political tipping points and natural tipping points. Can we close coal-fired power plants fast enough to save the Greenland ice sheet? Can we halt the deforestation of the Amazon rainforest before the ongoing clearing of land so weakens the forest that it becomes vulnerable to natural fire and disappears, releasing vast amounts of carbon into the atmosphere?

Can we cut carbon emissions fast enough to save at least the larger glaciers in the Himalayas and on the Tibetan plateau? Can we shift from an energy economy powered largely by fossil fuels to one powered largely by wind, solar, and geothermal energy as some small countries are already doing, before we reach the point of no return?

The U.S. World War II Mobilization Model

Whenever I begin to feel overwhelmed by the scale and urgency of the changes we need to make, I reread the economic history of U.S. involvement in World War II because it is such an inspiring example of rapid mobilization. Initially, the United States resisted involvement in the war and responded only after it was directly attacked by Japan at Pearl Harbor. But respond it did.

In his State of the Union address on January 6, 1942, one month after the bombing of Pearl Harbor, President Franklin D. Roosevelt announced the country's arms production goals. The United States, he said, was planning to produce 45,000 tanks, 60,000 planes, and thousands of ships. He added, "Let no man say it cannot be done." No one had ever seen such huge arms production numbers. Public skepticism abounded. But Roosevelt and his colleagues realized that the world's largest single concentration of industrial power at that time was in the U.S. automobile industry. Even during the Depression, the United States was producing 3 million or more cars a year.

After his State of the Union address, Roosevelt met with auto industry leaders, indicating that the country would rely heavily on them to reach these arms production goals. Initially they expected to continue making cars and simply add on the production of armaments. What they did not know was that the sale of new cars would soon be banned. From early 1942 through the end of 1944, nearly three years, essentially no cars were produced in the United States.

Yet 1942 witnessed the greatest expansion of industrial output in the nation's history—all for military use. The United States far exceeded the initial goal of 60,000 planes, turning out a staggering 229,600 aircraft, a fleet so vast it is hard even today to visualize it. Equally impressive, by the end of the war more than 5,000 ships were added to the 1,000 or so that made up the American Merchant Fleet when the war began.

In retrospect, the speed of this conversion from a peacetime to a wartime economy is stunning. The harnessing of U.S. industrial power tipped the scales decisively toward the Allied Forces, reversing the tide of war. Nazi Germany and Imperial Japan, already fully extended, could not counter this effort.

It did not take decades to restructure the U.S. industrial economy. It did not take years. It was done in a matter of months. If we could restructure the U.S. industrial economy in months, then we can restructure the world energy economy during this decade. With numerous U.S. automobile assembly plants currently idled, it would be a relatively simple matter to retool them to produce wind turbines, as the Ford Motor Company did in World War II when it converted its Willow Run plant assembly line to produce B-24 bombers. This would help the world see that the economy can be restructured quickly, profitably, and in a way that enhances global security.

Looking for a Leader

The world now has the technologies and financial resources to stabilize climate, eradicate poverty, stabilize population, restore the economy's natural support systems, and, above all, restore hope. The United States, the wealthiest society that has ever existed, has the resources to lead this effort.

We can calculate roughly the costs of the changes needed to move our 21st century civilization off the decline-and-collapse path and onto a path that will sustain civilization. For less than $200 billion of additional funding per year worldwide, we can get rid of hunger, illiteracy, disease, and poverty; we can stabilize population; and we can restore the Earth's soils, forests, and fisheries. We can build a global community where the basic needs of virtually all people are satisfied—a world that will allow us to think of ourselves as civilized.

Just as the forces of decline can reinforce each other, so too can the forces of progress. For example, shifting from fossil fuels to renewable sources of energy obviously reduces carbon emissions, but it also reduces air pollution. Eradicating poverty accelerates the shift to smaller families. Reforestation sequesters carbon, increases aquifer recharge, and reduces soil erosion. Once we get enough trends headed in the right direction, they will reinforce each other.

Saving civilization means adopting Plan B and doing it at wartime speed. We cannot say we do not understand the dangers of the situation we're in or the urgency of reversing the trends that are undermining civilization. We do. We cannot say we do not have the resources. We do.

What is needed now is leadership. It's unlikely that civilization can be saved unless the United States leads in that effort. And that, Mr. President, brings the challenge to you. Just as the United States, led by President Roosevelt, decisively turned the tide in World War II, so, too, the United States led by you, has inherited the responsibility of saving civilization. In the 1940s the challenge was to save the democratic way of life. Today the stakes are far higher. It is civilization itself that is hanging in the balance.

Lester R. Brown, whom the Washington Post praised as "one of the world's most influential thinkers," built his understanding of the environment from the ground up. His entrepreneurial skills surfaced early working on the family's farm in southern New Jersey. Even while excelling in school, he launched with his younger brother a tomato growing operation that by 1958 was producing 1.5 million pounds of tomatoes.

While on a brief assignment for the USDA (US Department of Agriculture) in India in 1965, he pieced together the early clues of an impending famine. His urgent warning to the U.S. and Indian governments set in motion the largest food rescue effort in history, saving millions of lives. This near-miss by India led it to adopt new agricultural policies that he helped to shape.

Lester Brown went on to advise governments internationally. For example, his 1995 book *Who Will Feed China?* led to a broad restructuring of China's agricultural policy.

He founded the Worldwatch Institute in 1974 and the Earth Policy Institute in 2001, two major non-profit environmental research organizations. Through these organizations and his writings, including

51 books published in 42 languages, Brown has helped us understand the interconnections between such issues as overpopulation, water shortages and climate change, and their effect on food security.

Never one to focus only on the problem, he always proposes pragmatic solutions to stave off the unfolding ecological crises that endanger our future. He has clearly laid out an eco-economy, and how to get from here to there. His plan to save civilization—Plan B—has four components: stabilize population, eradicate poverty, cut carbon emissions by 80 percent, and restore the economy's natural support systems, including forests, grasslands, and fisheries.

From a poor, but ambitious young man to a scholar and leader, Lester Brown inspires people to be all they can be. He states: "I was born at home in a small house for hired hands nine miles west of Bridgeton, New Jersey, on March 28, 1934. During the early years, when we were sharecropping, our home had no electricity, no running water or indoor plumbing, and no refrigerator. Mom cooked on a woodstove. She washed our clothes on a washboard in a metal tub in which we took our baths once a week. By age five I was doing daily chores, including cleaning out the horse stables."

In his latest book, *Breaking New Ground: A Personal History*, Brown recounts his life story as one of the founders of the global environmental movement. He recognized the process of globalization well before the term existed and helped define sustainable development. Brown spent his life analyzing the state of the planet through an interdisciplinary lens. The first in his family to graduate from elementary school, he reveals what inspired him—and the millions who have read his books—to become environmentally active.

Capitalism: Growth, Greed and Collapse
by Lindsey Grant

"Anyone who believes exponential growth can go on forever in a finite world is either a madman or an economist."
— Economist Kenneth Boulding, 1977

If there were one message I could imprint on the American mind, it would be this: Perpetual physical growth is impossible on a finite planet.... the question inescapably becomes, not should human growth stop? but when? How should it stop? by conscious efforts to limit fertility, or by rising mortality?... The distinguishing characteristic of this century is that growth has reached the point at which this choice has become an immediate issue. (*Juggernaut: Growth on a Finite Planet*, 1996)

I wrote that paragraph 18 years ago, and the only change I would now make is to change the tense. Deploying the techniques of Capitalism and new technologies in food production and public health, we have engineered an astounding growth in human populations and their demands on Earth's resources. We have entered the zone of overshoot, in which those resources are insufficient to maintain the populations dependent upon them, and human overload is damaging the biosphere and reducing the Earth's capacity to support us and other creatures.

In humans' brief time on Earth, various civilizations have

pursued growth with Darwinian enthusiasm, and crashed when they ran through their resources. None has grown so spectacularly as the worldwide system of Capitalism, and none has faced a systemic collapse as total as the world economy now faces.

Capitalism and Growth

Capitalism dates from the 1700s. Its unique institutions are private ownership of the means of production for private profit, and a labor market working for the capitalists for hourly wages. That structure freed the capitalists from any obligation to labor other than the payment of whatever wage the market required, and it generated a hostile class confrontation. However, it also organized the industrial revolution, led to the effective employment of new technologies: steam power, and then electricity and commercial agriculture. The capitalists sought free trade to create larger markets and open new sources of food and raw materials. Economies of scale brought improved managerial techniques. Together, the innovations led to a period of growth unlike anything in previous history, and those who prospered came to believe in growth as the natural order of society.

Population growth took off at the same time. The curve has been astonishing. From about 500 million in 1700, world population has now passed 7.1 billion, a thirteen-fold growth in twelve generations—and 85 percent of that growth has occurred since 1900.

As its money and political power grew, Capitalism created the legal system and the machinery to drive growth without the acceptance of its limits. The institutions of capitalism are designed to promote economic growth, and they succeeded.

- The limited liability corporation loads the odds in favor of the entrepreneur who takes risks in the pursuit of growth. If he fails, he loses only the money he put in the corporation, and usually not all of that.
- Starting in 1933, the major governments of the world abandoned the gold standard and with it the principal restraint on the formation of capital. Money is now created by fiat at the whim of governments and central banks. ("QE"—quantitative easing—is the current euphemism for the machinery whereby the Fed creates money and pumps it into the business sector—$1 trillion per year, created out of the thin air.) Capital is no longer the limiting factor in investment. The only proximate constraint is the question: does the proposal

promise high profits to the money lenders?

- The modern banking system rests upon leverage—the ability to issue more money in loans than the banks possess. Even regulated banks are allowed leverage of 5:1 of more, and there are essentially no controls on private banks other than their ability to find borrowers.
- The U.S. tax system is rigged to impose lower taxes on capital gains than on regular income, thus creating the situation that Warren Buffet recently described: he is one of the richest people in the country, and his tax rate is lower than his secretary's.
- Even the fear of inflation does not deter the sturdy capitalist. The Fed and other central banks welcome inflation up to a point—usually 2% or 4% per annum—because it enables risk takers (and Treasuries) to pay off their debts in depreciated money, even as it systematically devalues the wealth of the cautious investor.

Add to that various Supreme Court decisions, notably *Citizens United* in 2010 and *McCutcheon v FEC* in 2014 that have increased companies' opportunities to influence legislation.

The profit motive leads to overbuilding, because there is more profit to be made in tearing down and building anew than in maintenance. The capitalist has an interest in population growth because it means larger markets, cheaper labor, and new construction. Growing populations need more schools, roads, bridges and other infrastructure.

The system is essentially a series of inverted pyramids, and as unstable as that metaphor suggests. It was designed for growth, not for stability. We learn that, from time to time, most recently in 2008. There is a self-evident reason for its existence: it serves the powerful. Economic Establishments everywhere have a stake in it. Every major national and international meeting on economic policy calls for more growth, as do the economists who serve them. It has been enormously profitable for Establishments, and greed urges them to keep the faith. The enthusiasm crosses party lines.

Even John Maynard Keynes called "The Problem of Population … the greatest of all social issues…" and castigated the "avarice and usury and precaution" that drives Capitalism.

What worked at the beginning failed with the growth of the system itself.

Cracks in the Edifice

The benefits of Capitalism turned sour as its scale and power grew. The fatal flaw was that the system depended upon the ever-increasing use of natural resources—which are finite—and upon the intentional or inadvertent destruction of life systems—which may be essential to humans—to support its own growth.

As to the use of resources: petroleum fueled the dramatic growth of the 20th Century, and it is the most conspicuous example of resource depletion. From 1950 to 1970, U.S. consumption of petroleum rose more than 4% per year. At that rate it would be 92 million barrels per day by now—five times our actual present consumption. It would have reached the absurdity of 1.3 billion barrels per day in another 63 years. We were warned. In 1953, petroleum geologist M. King Hubbert predicted that U.S. crude oil production would peak in 1970, at the latest. It did peak, right on schedule. Alaskan oil did not save us, nor will fracking. We have changed the definition of "petroleum" by adding natural gas liquids and biofuels to crude oil, but even by that definition per capita petroleum consumption has fallen to 70 percent of its 1978 peak. The U.S. has gone from the illusion of plenty to the reality of Peak Oil, and other countries are following similar trajectories.

Petroleum is hardly unique. Christopher Clugston in his new book *Scarcity* studied 89 of the non-renewable, non-energy minerals tracked by the USGS and concluded that 63 of them are already scarce, worldwide. His calculations were conservative. At some time, the use of any non-renewable resource will taper off as the cost of extracting it rises. We had better learn a lot, very quickly, about recycling.

Banks and governments can create fiat money, but they cannot reverse that downward curve of mineral accessibility. Growth apologists take refuge in the myth of "infinite substitutability". In this case, resources being short and capital infinitely expansible, they argue that capital can be substituted for resources, or for labor in the form of automation. (And then they fire the workers.) However, Herman Daly, a more prudent economist, points out that you cannot maintain lumber production by building more lumber mills after you have cut the forest down. Resources and capital are complementary inputs, not substitutes.

Indeed, capital can be used to buy mines and land, and to grow trees. The problem is, with increasing scarcities, the capital buys less and less. There is a name for that phenomenon: inflation.

Fresh water resources are on the borderline between renewable and non-renewable. Try to name a substitute. Don't name "salt water", because desalination requires a lot of energy, and energy is getting scarcer and more expensive. There is no meaningful substitute for fresh water.

As to our disturbance of natural systems: we dispose of wastes without regard to the harm they do—until they pollute the air, water and the land, or drive changes in the climate, at levels we cannot ignore. Rising human activity changes natural systems. Watch the climate change, with deeper drought and wilder storms, acidification of the oceans, and intense heat in lower latitudes as we capture more solar energy. Think of the loss of natural forests, or the degrading of soils under modern commercial agriculture, or urban growth supplanting farmland and natural grasslands.

We must reverse human degradation of the biosphere. Humans are causing one of the major extinction events in the history of life on the planet.

Those realities have begun to show up in the U.S. economy since the 1970s. We are running on momentum.

- Real hourly wages are now slightly below those of the 1970s, and households have maintained their living style only with rising debt. U.S. GDP, adjusted for inflation, has managed to stay just ahead of population growth, but the progress is illusory, because all the income growth has gone to the wealthiest 1 percent of families.

- We have moved from the production of real goods to low-wage "services", and to the financial sector, much of which is of little benefit except to the gamblers involved. Manufacturing employment has declined 39 percent since 1978.

- Food, raw materials, minerals and energy prices have surged in the past decade, despite a major crash and a sluggish economy. They are pulling the consumer price index upward.

- As a nation, we have moved from the world's largest creditor to its largest debtor.

- A growing economy requires a growing infrastructure, and we are not maintaining what we have.

- Unemployment is the worst immediate problem, because it destroys people's sense of a meaningful role in society. Forget the conventional unemployment statistics. The real issue is how many people have jobs. We are in the midst of a crisis.

Employment peaked at 146 million in 2007, dropped in 2008 and is now back up to142 million. Our pundits applaud any increase in the number, but they forget that we must keep running to stay in the same place. The civilian population over 16 years old has risen 12 million since 2007. The percentage employed has dropped from 63% to 58.6%, which suggests that we need 10 million new jobs to match the employment level of 2007.

• That, and the growing income gap, have led to rising resentment of the rich. In 1928, the top 1 percent of income earners received 23.9 percent of all income. That declined steadily for decades, until in 1975 the figure was down to 8.9 percent. In other words, wage earners were getting more of a growing pie. It was a quiet, massive social revolution, started by the New Deal. That turned around in the Reagan years, and by 2007 the top 1 percent were back up to 23.5 percent of total income. After a brief dip in 2008 it is back to that level, and still rising. And the distribution of wealth is much more skewed than income.

How have our "leaders" dealt with it? By promoting "immigration reform" that seeks to bring in more labor to compete for scarce jobs and thus push wages down and unemployment up. Precisely the wrong "solution" for a huge problem. We need to bring the supply of labor back down in line with the demand.

A Question of Food

The present problems are just the beginning. Worldwide, the most pressing single issue is food. A world population of 7.1 billion is now supported by the same acreage of arable land that supported 2.5 billion in 1950. How? Primarily because we have learned to use fossil fuel to extract nitrogen from the air for fertilizer. We found massive deposits of phosphates in Morocco and Florida, and potash in Canada. We used pumps to exploit groundwater aquifers, and irrigation multiplied. We launched the "green revolution" with new crop strains.

We are running out of those solutions. They are drying up (literally, in the case of water). Without those inputs, the "green revolution" withers away. Climate change threatens food production. Without fossil fuels, we will need to use more arable land for draft animals and fertilizer.

Unless human populations can be brought down as food supplies decline, we face starvation. Something may turn up, as Mr. Micawber used to say, but don't bet on it. Scientists have been seeking new ways to maintain food output, such as nitrogen-fixing microbes on grains, but after 60 years they have not succeeded.

As a rule of thumb, one might look at the population the Earth supported before the spread of those technical innovations. The answer: less than 2.5 billion. That might be a good target, assuming that the damage we have done since then cancels out the gains we have made in plant breeding. It may still be too high, if soil productivity cannot be maintained at that level, or if we encounter some incalculable threats—think of the Irish Famine.

Food is only one issue. For another one: the shift from fossil to renewable energy will require investments unprecedented in human history, and in a time of rising raw material and energy prices.

We are facing a world in turmoil as the competition grows for diminishing resources and jobs. The interminable wars in East Africa and the Middle East are regarded as ethnic or religious conflicts, but they are generated at least in part by economic desperation. They may be the models for the next century. The Syrian civil war was triggered by a drought.

The Finite Earth Paradigm

We badly need a completely new view of humankind on Earth. We must diminish our disturbance of Earth systems, not multiply it. Fewer people. Leaner economies. Action on anthropogenic climate change. Only by accepting and adopting the vision of a finite Earth can we save the human tribe from an increasingly desperate future.

Such changes are unimaginable without a dramatic shift from the unbridled pursuit of individual gain, with its intensifying class and group antagonisms, to an ethical belief system that puts the sense of community above greed, and wellbeing above growth. And the community is the living Earth.

From Turmoil, A Distant Hope

It is probably too late to avoid a time of chaos. Unemployment will probably get worse, and there is little prospect of avoiding a food calamity until—one way or another—populations decline along with food production.

But things have been tough before, and people have lived

through it. Humans make a lot of mistakes, but we do learn—slowly. Worldwide, the average total fertility rate has declined from 5.0 children to 2.4 in 60 years. That decline is remarkable evidence that—even without governmental "leadership" —people can learn to adjust to an urbanizing world in which children are a financial burden rather than an asset. That decline must continue.

The problem here is that we have still learned only half the solution. Many of the poorest countries, mostly in Africa, still have fertility rates of five or more children. The U.N. Population Division projects that the 58 "high fertility" countries' population will rise from 1.2 billion now to 4.2 billion by 2100, and from 18 percent of world population to 42 percent—and even that calculation requires an heroic decline in fertility from 4.9 children to 2.1 by 2100. I don't think the numbers will get there, or anywhere near it, because starvation will drive mortality up. Those people will be desperate to migrate to less impoverished lands.

What can we do to avoid being inundated by immigration? The issue is particularly poignant if we develop a sense of community, and the Earth is the community. Do we allow a portion of the world's people to starve? Can we prevent it? Or do we starve with them? Can they learn to manage their own fertility, very quickly? We can try (as we have tried) to help them to pursue lower fertility. But it is hugely difficult to undertake such social engineering in societies that are close to anarchy. And the prosperous countries are going to be in deep trouble, themselves, in the coming century.

Migration will not solve the problems; it will cause them to metastasize. The more prosperous nations may well decide to protect ourselves by defending our borders, but it would be a heartrending and partial solution.

As I said: tumultuous times.

What I have to offer may seem thoroughly unsatisfactory to many readers, but it may be the best we can do. Think very long term, and don't be mired in despair. We may be in for troubled times, but it may teach us to move on to a new balance with the Earth. Given the damage we are doing to our support systems, that balance may require a world population of one billion or less, not 2.5 billion. We were there before, three centuries ago, and in retrospect it looks like a livable number. It might be rather pleasant, after our present overcrowded condition. I would add that that level could be truly sustainable. The human extraction of minerals and fossil energy was, by modern standards, negligible in 1700.

I don't imagine that human nature is going to change, but there is some evidence that we can learn. We need to learn to think as a community and recognize our shared interest in reversing the growth that threatens all of us.

Portions of this article were published in October 2013 by Negative Population Growth, Inc.

Lindsey Grant was born in Chapel Hill, North Carolina in 1926 and raised mostly in Bronxville, New York and St. Simons Island, Georgia. He attended Deep Springs College in California, served as an Ensign in the Navy in World War II, and graduated from Cornell University, where he was a member of Telluride Association. He became a U.S. Foreign Service Officer and China specialist. He met his future wife, Burwell Marshall, in Hong Kong in 1951.

As Director of the Office of Asian Communist Affairs in the U.S. Department of State, he drafted Assistant Secretary of State Roger Hilsman's Commonwealth Club speech of December 1962, which was the first public statement by the U.S. Government that we expected to live with Communist China, not to overthrow it.

As a National Security Council (NSC) staff member, he proposed and drafted the "Nixon Doctrine", in which the President said that henceforth the United States planned to provide a shield to friendly countries against aggression, but that it was up to them, not us, to provide their people with healthy societies resistant to aggression. This doctrine became an important part of President Nixon's basic foreign policy statement, *U.S. Foreign Policy for the 1970s*. It was, regrettably, abandoned by subsequent Presidents.

During those years, Grant became convinced that world population growth and its environmental impacts were more important issues than bilateral foreign policy. As Deputy Assistant Secretary of State for Environment and Population Affairs, he was the initiator and Department of State coordinator for the *Global 2000 Report* to President Carter. He chaired the Interagency Committee on International Environmental Affairs, was the U.S. delegate to (and Vice Chairman of) the OECD Environment Committee, U.S. member of a United Nations Committee of Experts on the Environment, and the initiator and convener of the first studies leading to international agreements on stratospheric ozone and on acid precipitation.

Mr. Grant retired from the Department of State in 1978 to become one of the small group of writers who have labored to persuade the country that population growth threatens the well-being and perhaps the existence of our society. His books include *Foresight and National Decisions: the Horseman and the Bureaucrat* (1988), *Elephants in the Volkswagen* (a study of optimum U.S. population, 1992), *How Many Americans?* (with Leon Bouvier, 1994), *Juggernaut: Growth on a Finite Planet* (1996), *Too Many People. The Case for Reversing Growth* (2001), *The Collapsing Bubble: Growth and Fossil Energy* (2005), and *Valedictory: The Age of Overshoot* (2007). Most of these books and dozens of his articles may be found at (www.npg.org) the website of Negative Population Growth, Inc.

As an amateur photographer, Grant participated in the Corcoran Gallery Biennial in 1978 and in the Department of State's Artists in Embassies program.

He has lived since 1992 in Santa Fe, New Mexico.

96

Shortages of Natural Resources Will Limit Human Population Numbers in the Future
by David Pimentel and Marcia Pimentel

More than 66 percent of the world's population is malnourished and the numbers are growing. Shortage of food because of limits of cropland, water, and other natural resources is the problem. In about 100 years when the planet runs out of fossil energy, we anticipate that the world population numbers will decline and be limited to about 2 billion people. After this decline, the U.S. population will be limited to about 100 million people.

World Overpopulation

Human population numbers is the problem that no one wants deal with. The current world population is estimated to be about 7.3 billion people. Based on the current rate of increase of 1.2 percent per year, the world population will double in 58 years. Thus, the current world population is projected to double to approximately 14.4 billion in less than 60 years. In general, we agree with the opinion that the world population will not double again for many reasons. The major constraint that is seldom mentioned is growing food shortages.

According to the World Health Organization (WHO) currently 4 billion humans are malnourished—the largest number ever. Food production is becoming limited because of shortages of cropland, fresh water, shortages of fertilizers that depend on fossil energy either for their production (nitrogen) or mining and processing (i.e., phosphorus, potassium, and micronutrients). These resource shortages are increasing along with the rapid growth in human population numbers throughout the world. The resource shortages and severity of malnutrition are most serious in Africa and Asia, the same places where population growth is the greatest.

Energy and Power

The real problem facing humans is the decline of oil production due to the exhaustion of reserves projected to occur in the next 30 to 40 years. The resource shortages impacted by the decline in oil supply and increase in oil prices will impact human health and survival in many ways but especially with the production of food.

The Foundation for Future projects that the world population will decline from the current 7.3 billion to only 2 billion in the next 100 years when oil, natural gas, and coal disappear. There will be few renewable energy sources to replace fossil energy sources as we now use them.

Currently there is talk about using biofuels from food crops, but using crops for fuel is already contributing to food shortages and starvation. One might use some wood material as an energy source in a few locations. But wood resources are already in short supply for lumber, fuel and other uses. Other resources that will help include water power, photovoltaics, solar thermal, and wind energy. One goal is to convert cellulose into ethanol fuel, but this has not been successful to date. The conversion into fuel to date has been less 0.1%.

Micronutrient Deficiencies

Micronutrient deficiencies are a serious problem for preschool and school children and pregnant women. Current estimates suggest that more than 870 million people, making up slightly more than 13 percent of the global population, are undernourished, and 852 million of these live in developing countries. According to the Food and Agriculture Organization (UN FAO) about 180 million children under 5 years of age are permanently stunted due to poor nutrition, while "wasting" is reported for nearly 60 million children.

Deficiencies in iron, iodine, vitamin A and zinc are reported to be more damaging and affect mostly pregnant women, primarily of reproductive age. Vitamin A, iron, and iodine deficiencies have been identified as public health problems in many Asian countries. Despite efforts to reduce the number of children suffering from malnutrition in developing countries, these diseases still continue to affect a large number of children who still suffer from poor health. They also suffer from low cognitive productivity and performance.

There is no question that micronutrient deficiencies reduce productivity and economic growth, and increase poverty by increasing health and intellectual problems, especially among children of school age. Estimates suggest that the costs of micronutrient deficiencies mount up to several billion dollars per year. These costs are most severe in developing countries where the depressed economic situation is already critical and persistent.

The public health of the world needs to give greater attention to the public health problems of developing countries. Greater effort must be given to reducing population numbers while improving agriculture and nutrition of the young.

Nothing Grows Forever

Some people are starting to ask just how many humans the Earth can support if we want to cease degrading the environment, stop using fossil fuels and move to a sustainable solar energy system. There is no solid answer yet, but the best estimate is that Earth can support about 1 to 2 billion people with an American Standard of Living, including good health, nutrition, prosperity, personal dignity, freedom and open space.

Because human population growth will be limited, will it be by natural forces such as disease and malnutrition? Or will it be by appropriate actions we choose ourselves?

This planet's numerous environmental problems highlight the urgent need to evaluate available land, water, and energy resources and how they relate to the requirements of a rapidly growing human population. We suggest appropriate policies and technologies that would improve standards of living and quality of life worldwide, while stabilizing population as rapidly as possible. These policies should be implemented soon. If we are not brave enough to limit our numbers, nature will impose its own limits on our numbers and our existence.

David Pimentel is a professor emeritus of ecology at the College of Agriculture and Life Sciences in Cornell University, Ithaca, New York. His PhD is from Cornell University. He did post-doctoral research at the University of Chicago and had a fellowship at Oxford University in England. Among other achievements in a long and distinguished career, he was awarded an honorary degree from the University of Massachusetts.

His research and consulting accomplishments cut across many disciplines, spanning the fields of energy, population ecology, human population growth, biological pest control, sustainable agriculture, land and water conservation and environmental policy. Pimentel has published more than 700 scientific papers and 40 books, and has served on many national and government committees; National Academy of Sciences; President's Science Advisory Council; U.S. Department of Agriculture; U.S. Department of Energy; U.S. Department of Health, Education and Welfare; Office of Technology Assessment of the U.S. Congress; and the U.S. State Department.

Pimentel's interest in human population developed while chairing studies on human, vertebrate, and invertebrate populations for the National Academy of Sciences. In addition, while with the U.S. Public Health Service, he devoted four years to investigating the control of the Indian mongoose in Puerto Rico. The mongeese were a threat to the island ecology, and they also spread diseases (rabies and others) to humans and to other animals.

Marcia Pimentel is a professor of Food Science at the College of Agriculture and Life Sciences in Cornell University, Ithaca, New York. Her Masters degree is from Cornell University. She has published more than 60 scientific papers, and four books, including *Dimensions of Food*. She is the joint author with David Pimentel of *Food, Energy, and Society*. She taught for 35 years in the College of Human Ecology. She has significant interest in human population growth and nutrition, and includes those subjects in her courses.

Marcia first became interested in population issues and food security while studying and teaching the dimensions and quality of food relative to numbers of people. She saw these dimensions first-hand while living in Puerto Rico for four years.

Can a Collapse of Global Civilization be Avoided?
by Paul R. Ehrlich and Anne H. Ehrlich

Virtually every past civilization has eventually undergone collapse, a loss of socio-political-economic complexity usually accompanied by a dramatic decline in population size. Some, like those of Egypt and China, have recovered from collapses at various stages; others, like that of Easter Island or the Classic Maya, were apparently permanent. All those previous collapses were local or regional; elsewhere other societies and civilizations persisted unaffected. Sometimes, as in the Tigris and Euphrates valleys, new civilizations rose in succession. In many if not most cases, overexploitation of the environment was one cause.

But today for the first time, humanity's *global* civilization—the worldwide, increasingly interconnected, highly technological society in which we all are to one degree or another, embedded—is threatened with collapse by an array of environmental problems. Humankind finds itself engaged in what Prince Charles described as "an act of suicide on a grand scale", facing what Britain's Chief Scientific Advisor John Beddington called a "perfect storm" of environmental problems. The most serious of these problems show signs of rapidly escalating severity, especially climate disruption. But other elements could potentially also contribute to a collapse: an accelerating extinction of animal and plant populations and species, which could lead to a loss of ecosystem services essential for human survival; land degradation and land-use change; a pole-to-pole spread of toxic compounds; ocean acidification and eutrophication (dead zones); worsening of some aspects of the epidemiological environment (factors that make human populations susceptible to infectious diseases); depletion of increasingly scarce resources, including especially groundwater, which is being overexploited in many key agricultural areas; water wars and other resource wars. These are not separate problems; rather they interact in two gigantic complex adaptive systems: the biosphere system and the human socio-economic system. The negative manifestations of these interactions are often referred to as "the human predicament", and determining how to prevent it from generating a global collapse is perhaps *the* foremost challenge confronting humanity.

The human predicament is driven by overpopulation, overconsumption of natural resources, and the use of unnecessarily environmentally damaging technologies and socio-economic-political arrangements to service *Homo sapiens'* aggregate consumption. How far the human population size now is above the planet's long-term carrying capacity is suggested (conservatively) by ecological footprint analysis. It shows that to support *today's* population of seven billion sustainably (that is, with business as usual, including current technologies and standards of living) would require roughly half an additional planet; **if all citizens of Earth consumed resources at the U.S. level, it would take four to five more Earths**.

Adding the projected 2.5 billion more people by 2050 would make the human assault on civilization's life-support systems disproportionately worse, since almost everywhere people face systems with nonlinear responses, in which environmental damage increases at a rate that becomes faster with each additional person.

Of course, the claim is often made that humanity will expand Earth's carrying capacity dramatically with technological innovation, but it is widely recognized that technologies can both add and subtract from carrying capacity. The plow evidently first expanded it and now appears to be reducing it. Overall, careful analysis of the prospects does not provide much confidence that technology will save us, or that GDP can be disengaged from resource use.

Do current trends portend a collapse?

What is the likelihood that this set of interconnected predicaments will lead to a global collapse in this century? There have been many definitions and much discussion of past "collapses", but a future global collapse does not require careful definition. It could be triggered by anything from a "small" nuclear war, whose ecological effects could quickly end civilization, to a more gradual breakdown because famines, epidemics, and resource shortages cause a disintegration of central control within nations, in concert with disruptions of trade and conflicts over increasingly scarce necessities. In either case, regardless of survivors or replacement societies, the world familiar to anyone reading this paper and the well-being of the vast majority of people would disappear.

How likely is such a collapse to occur? No civilization can avoid collapse if it fails to feed its population. The world's success so far, and the prospective ability to feed future generations at least as well, has been under relatively intensive discussion for a half-century. Agriculture made civilization possible and, over the last 80 years or so, an industrial agricultural revolution has created a technology-dependent global food system. That system, humanity's single biggest industry, has generated miracles of food production. But it has also created serious long-run vulnerabilities, especially in its dependence on stable climates, crop monocultures, industrially produced fertilizers and pesticides, petroleum, antibiotic feed supplements, and rapid, efficient transportation.

Despite those food production miracles, today at least two billion people are hungry or poorly nourished. The FAO estimates that increasing food production by some 70% would be required to feed a 35% bigger and still growing human population adequately by 2050. What are the prospects that *Homo sapiens* can produce and distribute sufficient food? To do so, it probably will be necessary to accomplish many or all of the following tasks: severely limit climate disruption; restrict expansion of land area for agriculture (to preserve ecosystem services); raise yields where possible; put much more effort into soil conservation; increase efficiency in use of fertilizers, water, and energy; become more vegetarian; grow more food for people (not fuel for vehicles); reduce food wastage; stop degradation of the oceans and better regulate aquaculture; significantly increase investment in sustainable agricultural and aquacultural research; and move increasing equity and feeding everyone to the very top of the policy agenda.

Most of these long-recommended tasks require changes in human behavior—thus far elusive.

The critical importance of substantially boosting the inadequate current action on the demographic problem can be seen in the time required to change the trajectory of population growth humanely and sensibly. We know from such things as the World War II mobilizations that many consumption patterns can be altered dramatically within a year, given appropriate incentives. Humane population stabilization and then reduction takes generations.

What needs to be done to avoid a collapse?

The threat from climate disruption to food production alone means that humanity's entire system for mobilizing energy needs to be rapidly transformed. Warming must be held well below a potential 5° C rise in global average temperature, a level that could well bring down civilization. The best estimate today may be that, failing rapid concerted action, the world is already committed to a 2.4°C increase in global average temperature. This is significantly above the 2°C estimated a decade ago by climate scientists to be a "safe" limit, but now considered by some analysts to be too dangerous, a credible assessment, given the effects seen already before reaching a one degree rise. There is evidence, moreover, that present models underestimate future temperature increase by overestimating the extent that growth of vegetation can serve as a carbon sink and underestimating positive feedback loops.

Many complexities plague estimation of the precise threats of anthropogenic climate disruption, ranging from heat deaths and spread of tropical diseases to sea-level rise, crop failures, and violent storms. One key to avoiding a global collapse, and thus an area requiring great effort and caution is avoiding climate-related mass famines. Our agricultural system evolved in a geologic period of relatively constant and benign climate and was well attuned to twentieth century conditions. That alone is cause for substantial concern as the planet's climates rapidly shift to new, less predictable regimes.

It is essential to slow that process. That means dramatically transforming much of the existing energy infrastructure and changing human behavior to make the energy system much more efficient. This *is* possible; indeed sensible plans for doing it have been put forward, and some progress has been made. The central challenge, of course, is to phase out more than half of the global use of fossil fuels by 2050 in order to forestall the worst impacts of climate disruption, a challenge the latest International Energy Agency edition of *World Energy Outlook* makes look more severe.

This highlights another dilemma. Fossil fuels are now essential to agriculture for fertilizer and pesticide manufacture, operation of farm machinery, irrigation (often wasteful), livestock husbandry, crop drying, food storage, transportation, and distribution. Thus the phase-out will need to include at least partial substitution of non-fossil fuels in these functions, and do so without greatly increasing food prices.

Unfortunately, essential steps such as curbing global emissions to peak by 2020 and reducing them to half of present levels by 2050 are extremely problematic economically and politically. Fossil fuel companies would have to leave most of their proven reserves in the ground, thus destroying much of the industry's economic value. Since the ethics of some businesses include knowingly continuing lethal but profitable activities, it is hardly surprising that interests with large financial stakes in fossil-fuel burning have launched a gigantic and largely successful disinformation campaign in the United States to confuse people about climate disruption and block attempts to deal with it.

One factor making the challenges more severe is the major participation in the global system of giant nations whose populations have not previously enjoyed the fossil energy abundance that brought western countries and Japan to positions of affluence. Now they are poised to repeat the West's energy "success," and on an even greater scale. India alone, which recently suffered a gigantic blackout affecting 300 million people, is planning to bring 455 new coal plants on line. Worldwide more than 1,200 plants with a total installed capacity of 1.4 million mega-watts are planned, much of that in China, where electricity demand is expected to skyrocket. The resultant surge in greenhouse gases will interact with the increasing diversion of grain to livestock, stimulated by the desire for more meat in the diets of Indians, Chinese, and others in a growing global middle class.

Dealing with problems beyond food supply

There is a real prospect of epidemics being enhanced by rapid population growth in immune-weakened societies, increased contact with animal reservoirs, high-speed transport, and the misuse of antibiotics. Nobel laureate Joshua Lederberg had great concern for the epidemic problem, famously stating, "The survival of the human species is not a preordained evolutionary program." Some precautionary steps that should be considered include forbidding the use of antibiotics as growth stimulators for livestock, building emergency stocks of key vaccines and drugs (such as Tamiflu), improving disease surveillance, expanding mothballed emergency medical facilities, preparing institutions for imposing quarantines, and, of course, moving as rapidly as possible to humanely reduce the human population size.

Another possible threat to the continuation of civilization is global toxification. Adverse symptoms of exposure to synthetic chemicals are making some scientists increasingly nervous about effects on the human population.

It has become increasingly clear that security has many dimensions beyond military security and that breaches of environmental security could risk the end of global civilization.

But much uncertainty about the human ability to avoid a collapse still hinges on military security, especially whether some elements of the human predicament might trigger a nuclear war. Recent research indicates that even a regional-scale nuclear conflict, as is quite possible between India and Pakistan, could lead to a global collapse through widespread climatic consequences. Triggers to conflict beyond political and religious strife easily could include cross-border epidemics, a need to gain access to food supplies and farmland, and competition over other resources, especially water and (if the world doesn't come to its energy senses) oil.

Finding ways to eliminate nuclear weapons and other instruments of mass destruction must move even higher on civilization's agenda, since nuclear war would be the quickest and surest route to a collapse.

In thinking about the probability of collapse, one must obviously consider the social disruptions associated with elements of the predicament. Perhaps at the top of the list should be that of environmental refugees. Recent predictions are that environmental refugees could number 50 million by 2020. Severe droughts, floods, famines, and epidemics could greatly swell that number. If current "official" predictions of sea-level rise are low (as many believe they are), coastal inundations alone could generate massive human movements; a one-meter rise would directly affect some 100 million people, whereas a six-meter rise would displace more than 400 million. Developing a more comprehensive system of international governance with institutions planning to ameliorate the impacts of such catastrophes would be a major way to reduce the odds of collapse.

The role of science

The scientific community has repeatedly warned humanity in the past of its peril, and the earlier warnings about the risks of population expansion and the "limits to growth" have increasingly been shown to be on the right track. The warnings continue. Yet many scientists still tend to treat population growth as an exogenous variable, when it should be considered an endogenous one—indeed, a central factor.

Too many studies asking "how can we possibly feed 9.6 billion people by 2050?" should also be asking "how can we humanely lower birth rates far enough to reduce that number to 8.6?" To our minds, the fundamental cure, reducing the scale of the human enterprise (including the size of the population) to keep its aggregate consumption within the carrying capacity of Earth, is obvious but too much neglected or denied. There are great social and psychological barriers in growthmanic cultures to even considering it. This is especially true because of the "endarkenment"—a rapidly growing movement toward religious orthodoxies that reject enlightenment values such as freedom of thought, democracy, separation of church and state, and basing beliefs and actions on empirical evidence. They are manifest in dangerous trends such as climate denial, failure to act on the loss of biodiversity, and opposition to condoms and other forms of contraception. If ever there was a time for evidence-based (as opposed to faith-based) risk reduction strategies, it is now.

How can scientists do more to reduce the odds of a collapse? Both natural and social scientists should put more effort into finding the best ways of accomplishing the necessary remodeling of energy and water infrastructure. The protection of Earth's remaining biodiversity must take center stage for both scientific specialists and, through appropriate education, the public. Scientists must continually call attention to the need to improve the human epidemiological environment, and for control and eventual elimination of nuclear, chemical, and biological weapons. Above all, they should expand efforts to understand the mechanisms through which cooperation evolves, since avoiding collapse will require unusual levels of international cooperation.

Is it too late for the global scientific community to collect itself and start to deal with the nexus of the two complex adaptive systems and then help generate the necessary actions to move toward sustainability? There are certainly many small-scale science-based efforts, often local, that can provide hope if scaled up. For example, environmental NGOs and others are continually struggling to halt the destruction of elements of biodiversity (and thus, in some cases, of vital ecosystem services), often with success. In the face of the building extinction crisis, they may be preserving nuclei from which Earth's biota and humanity's ecosystem services might eventually be regenerated. And some positive efforts *are* scaling up. China now has some 25 percent of its land in conservation areas designed to protect both natural capital and human well-being. The Natural Capital Project is helping improve the management of these areas. This is good news, but in our view, many too few scientists are involved in the efforts needed, especially in re-orienting at least part of their research toward mitigating the predicament and then bringing their results to the policy front.

The need for rapid social and political change

Until very recently, our ancestors had no reason to respond genetically or culturally to long-term issues. If the global climate were changing rapidly for *Australopithecus* or even ancient Romans, they were not causing it and could do nothing about it. The forces of genetic and cultural selection were not creating brains or institutions capable of looking generations ahead; there would have been no selection pressures in that direction. Indeed, quite the opposite; selection probably favored mechanisms to keep perception of the environmental background steady so that rapid changes (e.g., leopard approaching) would be obvious.

But now slow changes in that background are the most lethal threats. Societies have a long history of mobilizing efforts, making sacrifices and changes, to defeat an enemy at the gates, or even just to compete more successfully with a rival. But there is not much evidence of societies mobilizing and making sacrifices to meet gradually worsening conditions that threaten real disaster for future generations. Yet that is exactly the sort of mobilization we believe is required to avoid a collapse.

Perhaps the biggest challenge in avoiding collapse is convincing people, especially politicians and economists, to break this ancient mold and alter their behavior relative to the basic population-consumption drivers of environmental deterioration. We know that simply informing people of the scientific consensus on a serious problem does not ordinarily produce rapid change, either in institutional or individual behavior.

This is obviously true regarding reproduction and overconsumption, especially visible in what amounts to a cultural addiction to continued economic growth among the already wealthy. One might think that the mathematics of compound interest would have convinced everyone long ago that growth of an industrialized economy at 3.5% annually cannot long continue. Unfortunately, most "educated" people are immersed in a culture that does not recognize, in the real world, a short history (a few centuries) of exponential growth does not imply a long future of such growth.

Unfortunately, awareness among scientists that humanity is in deep trouble has not been accompanied by popular awareness and pressure to counter the political and economic influences implicated in the current crisis. Without significant pressure from the public demanding action, we fear there is little chance of changing course fast enough to forestall disaster.

The needed pressure, however, might be generated by a popular movement based in academia and civil society to help guide humanity toward developing a new multiple intelligence—"foresight intelligence"—to provide the long-term analysis and planning that markets cannot supply. Foresight intelligence could not only systematically look ahead but also guide cultural changes toward desirable outcomes such as increased socio-economic resilience. Helping develop such a movement and foresight intelligence are major challenges today.

If foresight intelligence became established, many more scientists and policy planners (and society) might, for example, understand the demographic contributions to the predicament, stop treating population growth as a "given" and consider the nutritional, health, and social benefits of humanely ending growth well below 9 billion and starting a slow decline. This would be a monumental task, considering the momentum of population growth. Monumental, but not impossible if the political will could be generated globally to give full rights, education, and opportunities to women, and provide all sexually active human beings with modern contraception and backup abortion. The degree to which those steps would reduce fertility rates is controversial, but they are a likely win-win for societies.

Obviously, especially with the growing endarkenment, there are huge cultural and institutional barriers to establishing such policies in some parts of the world. After all, there is not a single nation where women are truly treated as equal to men. Despite that, the population driver should not be ignored simply because limiting overconsumption can, at least in theory, be achieved more rapidly. The difficulties of changing demographic trajectories mean that the problem should have been addressed sooner, rather than later. That halting population growth inevitably leads to changes in age structure is no excuse for bemoaning drops in fertility rates, as is common in European government circles. Reduction of population size in those overconsuming nations is a very positive trend, and sensible planning can deal with the problems of population aging.

While rapid policy change to head off collapse is essential, fundamental institutional change to keep things on track is necessary as well. This is especially true of educational systems, which today fail to inform most people of how the world works and thus perpetuate a vast culture gap. The academic challenge is especially great for economists, who could help set the background for avoiding collapse by designing steady-state economic systems, and along the way destroying fables such as "growth can continue forever if it's in service industries," or "technological innovation will save us."

At the global level, the loose network of agreements that now tie countries together, developed in a relatively recent stage of cultural evolution since modern nation states appeared, is utterly inadequate to grapple with the human predicament. Strengthening global environmental governance and addressing the related problem of avoiding failed states are tasks humanity has so far refused to tackle comprehensively even as cultural evolution in technology has rendered the present international system (like educational systems) obsolete. Serious global environmental problems can only be solved and a collapse avoided with an unprecedented level of international cooperation. Regardless of one's estimate of civilization's potential longevity, the time to start restructuring the international system is right now. If people don't do that, nature will restructure civilization for us.

Similarly, widely based cultural change is required to reduce humanely both population size and overconsumption by the rich. Both go against cultural norms, and, as long feared, the overconsumption norm has understandably been adopted by the increasingly rich subpopulations of developing nations, notably India and China. One can be thrilled by the numbers of people raised from poverty while being apprehensive about the enormous and possibly lethal environmental and social costs that may result. The industrial revolution set civilization on the road to collapse, spurring population growth, which contributed slightly more than overconsumption to environmental degradation. Now population combined with affluence growth may finish the job.

Needless to say, dealing with economic and racial inequities will be critically important in getting large numbers of people from culturally diverse groups to focus their minds on solving the human predicament, something globalization should help. These tasks are being pursued, along with an emphasis on developing "foresight intelligence," by the *Millennium Alliance for Humanity and the Biosphere* "the MAHB" (mahb.stanford.edu). One of its central goals is to try to accelerate change towards sustainability. Since simply giving the scientific facts to the public won't do it, this means finding frames and narratives to convince the public of the need to make changes.

We know that societies can evolve fundamentally and unexpectedly, as was dramatically demonstrated by the collapse of communist regimes in Europe in 1989. Rather than tinkering around the edges and making feeble or empty gestures toward one or another of the interdependent problems we face, we need a powerful and comprehensive approach. In addressing climate change, for instance, developing nations need to be convinced that they (along with the rest of the world) cannot afford (and don't need) to delay action while they "catch up" in development. Indeed, development on the old model is counterproductive; they have a great opportunity to pioneer new approaches and technologies. All nations need to stop waiting for others to act and be willing to do everything they can to mitigate emissions and hasten the energy transition, regardless of what others are doing.

Can we avoid collapse?

Do we think global society can avoid a collapse in this century? The answer is yes, since modern society has shown some capacity to deal with long-term threats, at least if they are obvious or continuously brought to attention (think of the risks of nuclear conflict). Humanity has the assets to get the job done, but the odds of avoiding collapse seem small since the risks are clearly not obvious to most people and the classic signs of impending collapse, especially diminishing returns to complexity, are everywhere. One central psychological barrier to taking dramatic action is the distribution of costs and benefits through time: the costs up front, the benefits accruing largely to unknown people in the future. But whether we or more optimistic observers are correct, our own ethical values compel us to think the benefits to those future generations are worth struggling for, to increase at least slightly the chances of avoiding a dissolution of today's global civilization as we know it.

Portions of this article were published in the Procedings of the Royal Society B Biological Sciences *journal, January 2013.*

Paul R. Ehrlich has been a household name since the publication of his 1968 bestseller, *The Population Bomb.* He was born on May 29, 1932 in Philadelphia, Pennsylvania. He received his Ph.D. from the University of Kansas.

Co-founder with Peter H. Raven of the field of coevolution, Ehrlich has pursued long-term studies of the structure, dynamics, and genetics of natural butterfly populations. He has also been a pioneer in alerting the public to the problems of overpopulation, and in raising issues of population, resources, and the environment as matters of public policy.

Ehrlich is the Bing Professor of Population Studies, Professor of Biological Sciences at Stanford University, Stanford, California. In addition he is Chairman of the Board of Directors of the Center for Conservation Biology at Stanford University. He has been a Stanford University faculty member since 1959.

As a writer, Ehrlich is prolific. He has authored and coauthored some 950 scientific papers and articles in the popular press and over 35 books, including *The Population Bomb, The Process of Evolution, Ecoscience, The Machinery of Nature, Extinction, Earth, The Science of Ecology, The Birder's Handbook, New World/New Mind, The Population Explosion, Healing the Planet, Birds in Jeopardy, The Stork and the Plow, Betrayal of Science and Reason, A World of Wounds, Human Natures, Wild Solutions, On the Wings of Checkerspots, One with Nineveh* and *The Dominant Animal.* He continues to write articles and blogs today.

Ehrlich has appeared as a guest on many hundreds of TV and radio programs including some 20 appearances on Johnny Carson's Tonight Show; he also was a correspondent for NBC News. In addition, he has given hundreds of public lectures in the past 40 years.

Ehrlich is a fellow of the American Association for the Advancement of Science, the American Academy of Arts and Sciences, the American Philosophical Society, and a member of the National Academy of Sciences. He has received numerous honorary degrees, the John Muir Award of the Sierra Club, the Gold Medal Award of the World Wildlife Fund International, a MacArthur Prize Fellowship, the Crafoord Prize of the Royal Swedish Academy of Sciences, the Volvo Environmental Prize, the Heinz Award for the Environment, the United Nations' Sasakawa Environmental Prize, and the 1998 Tyler Prize for Environmental Achievement. Many of these honors he shares with his wife and collaborator, Anne H. Ehrlich.

Paul Ehrlich's 1968 book, *The Population Bomb*, was a wake-up call for an entire generation. By 1993, the Ehrlichs' perspective had become the consensus view of scientists as represented by the "World Scientists' Warning to Humanity" (Read the "Warning" in the Documents section of this book) and the statement issued by the Population Summit of the world's scientific academies in New Delhi.

Anne H. Ehrlich was born on November 17, 1933 in Des Moines, Iowa. She earned a bachelor's degree in biology from the University of Kansas. She is now a Senior Research Scientist in Biology at Stanford University, Stanford, California. She focuses her research on policy issues related to the environment. In 1987, she also became Associate Director/Policy Coordinator of the Center for Conservation Biology at Stanford.

Anne Ehrlich has carried out research and co-authored many technical articles in population biology. She also has written extensively on issues of public concern such as population and family planning, environmental protection, and environmental consequences of nuclear war—and is co-author of ten books, including *The Population Explosion, Healing the Planet, The Stork and the Plow,* and *Betrayal of Science and Reason*.

Anne served as one of seven consultants to The White House Council on Environmental Quality's *Global 2000 Report* (1980) and has served on the boards of directors of Friends of the Earth, Conferences on the Fate of the Earth, the Center for Innovative Diplomacy, Redefining Progress, and the editorial board of Pacific Discovery (journal of the California Academy of Sciences).

She is the recipient of the United Nations' Sasakawa Environment Prize, the Heinz Award for Environmental Achievement,

Distinguished Peace Leader Award from the Nuclear Age Peace Foundation, and the 1998 Tyler Prize for Environmental Achievement. Many of these honors she shares with her husband and collaborator, Paul Ehrlich.

Paul and Anne Ehrlich have worked together since the 1950s, beginning their scientific collaboration through research on butterflies. This led to an important understanding of the dynamics of animal populations.

These ecological and evolutionary principles were later applied by the Ehrlichs to help assess the impact of human populations on the environment. In examining the impacts of population growth, consumption, and use of inappropriate technologies around the world, the Ehrlichs have produced an enormous body of work—and stimulated public and political attention to environmental issues. They have displayed exceptional personal courage in taking a prominent public stand on diverse questions critical to the future of humankind, such as the preservation of biodiversity and endangered species, the hazards of pesticide pollution, the search for racial justice, and nuclear winter.

The Ehrlichs have together written more than 30 books and hundreds of articles.

The Ehrlichs remain active as leaders in scientific and environmental organizations. Most recently they have founded The MAHB: The Millennium Alliance for Humanity and the Biosphere. The MAHB mission is to foster, fuel and inspire a global dialogue on the interconnectedness of activities causing environmental degradation and social inequity—and to create and implement strategies for shifting human cultures and institutions towards sustainable practices, and an equitable and satisfying future.

Through the Center for Conservation Biology at Stanford, they work with an international team of scholars to use science to help conserve humanity's "biological capital." That capital is the plants, animals, and microorganisms that are essential to providing the ecosystem services that support human society.

III. Documents

World Leaders' Statement on Population Stabilization

Humankind has many challenges: to obtain a lasting peace between nations; to preserve the quality of the environment; to conserve natural resources at a sustainable level; to advance the economic and social progress of the less developed nations; to assure basic human rights and at the same time accept responsibility for the planet Earth and future generations of children; and to stabilize population growth.

Degradation of the world's environment, income inequality, and the potential for conflict exist today because of rapid population growth, among other factors. If this unprecedented population growth continues, future generations of children will not have adequate food, housing, health services, education, earth resources, and employment opportunities.

We believe that the time has come now to recognize the worldwide necessity to achieve population stabilization and for each country to adopt the necessary policies and programs to do so, consistent with its own culture and aspirations. To enhance the integrity of the individual and the quality of life for all, we believe that all nations should participate in setting goals and programs for population stabilization. Measures for this purpose should be voluntary and should maintain individual human rights and beliefs.

We urge national leaders to take an active personal role in promoting effective policies and programs. Emphasis should be given to improving the status of women, respecting human rights and beliefs, and achieving the active participation of women in formulating policies and programs. Attention should be given to realistic goals and timetables and developing appropriate economic and social policies.

Recognizing that early population stabilization is in the interest of all nations, we earnestly hope that leaders around the world will share our views and join with us in this great undertaking for the wellbeing and happiness of people everywhere.

The Statement has been signed by the heads of government of the following countries:

Austria
Bangladesh
Barbados
Bhutan
Botswana
Cape Verde
China, People's
  Republic
Colombia
Cyprus
Dominica
Dominican Republic
Egypt
Fiji
Gambia
Ghana
Grenada
Guinea-Bissau
Guyana
Haiti
Iceland
India
Indonesia
Israel
Jamaica
Jordan

Kenya
Korea, DPR
Korea
Republic of Laos
Liberia
Libya
Singapore
Malawi
Maldives
Malta
Suriname
Moldova
Morocco
Myanmar
Namibia
Nepal
Nigeria
Pakistan
Palau
Panama
Peru
Philippines
Rwanda
Saint Kitts and
  Nevis
Saint Lucia

Saint Vincent and
  the Grenadines
Saõ Tomé and
  Príncipe Senegal
Seychelles
Macedonia
Slovak Republic
Sri Lanka
Sudan
Mauritius
Swaziland
Tanzania
Thailand
Tonga, Kingdom of
Trinidad and Tobago
Tunisia
Turkey
Uganda
United Arab Emirates
Uzbekistan
Vanuatu
Zimbabwe

❖

Facing the Population Challenge

World Scientists' Warning to Humanity

Some 1,700 of the world's leading scientists, including the majority of Nobel laureates in the sciences, issued this appeal in November 1992. The World Scientists' Warning to Humanity was written and spearheaded by the late Henry Kendall, former chair of Union of Concerned Scientist's board of directors.

INTRODUCTION

Human beings and the natural world are on a collision course. Human activities inflict harsh and often irreversible damage on the environment and on critical resources. If not checked, many of our current practices put at serious risk the future that we wish for human society and the plant and animal kingdoms, and may so alter the living world that it will be unable to sustain life in the manner that we know. Fundamental changes are urgent if we are to avoid the collision our present course will bring about.

THE ENVIRONMENT

The environment is suffering critical stress:

The Atmosphere

Stratospheric ozone depletion threatens us with enhanced ultraviolet radiation at the Earth's surface, which can be damaging or lethal to many life forms. Air pollution and acid precipitation, are already causing widespread injury to humans, forests, and crops.

Water Resources

Heedless exploitation of depletable ground water supplies endangers food production and other essential human systems. Heavy demands on the world's surface waters have resulted in serious shortages in some 80 countries, containing 40 percent of the world's population. Pollution of rivers, lakes, and ground water further limits the supply.

Oceans

Destructive pressure on the oceans is severe, particularly in the coastal regions which produce most of the world's food fish. The total marine catch is now at or above the estimated maximum sustainable yield. Some fisheries have already shown signs of collapse. Rivers carrying heavy burdens of eroded soil into the seas also carry industrial, municipal, agricultural, and livestock waste—some of it toxic.

Soil

Loss of soil productivity, which is causing extensive land abandonment, is a widespread by-product of current practices in agriculture and animal husbandry. Since 1945, 11 percent of the Earth's vegetated surface has been degraded—an area larger than India and China combined—and per capita food production in many parts of the world is decreasing.

Forests

Tropical rain forests, as well as tropical and temperate dry forests, are being destroyed rapidly. At present rates, some critical forest types will be gone in a few years, and most of the tropical rain forest will be gone before the end of the next century. With them will go large numbers of plant and animal species.

Living Species

The irreversible loss of species, which by 2100 may reach one-third of all species now living, is especially serious. We are losing the potential they hold for providing medicinal and other benefits, and the contribution that genetic diversity of life forms gives to the robustness of the world's biological systems and to the astonishing beauty of the Earth itself. Much of this damage is irreversible on a scale of centuries, or permanent. Other processes appear to pose additional threats. Increasing levels of gases in the atmosphere from human activities, including carbon dioxide released from fossil fuel burning and from deforestation, may alter climate on a global scale. Predictions of global warming are still uncertain—with projected effects ranging from tolerable to very severe—but the potential risks are very great.

Our massive tampering with the world's interdependent web of life—coupled with the environmental damage inflicted by deforestation, species loss, and climate change—could trigger widespread adverse effects, including unpredictable collapses of critical biological systems whose interactions and dynamics we only imperfectly understand.

Uncertainty over the extent of these effects cannot excuse complacency or delay in facing the threats.

POPULATION

The Earth is finite. Its ability to absorb wastes and destructive effluent is finite. Its ability to provide food and energy is finite. Its ability to provide for growing numbers of people is finite. And we are fast approaching many of the Earth's limits. Current economic practices which damage the environment, in both developed and underdeveloped nations, cannot be continued without the risk that vital global systems will be damaged beyond repair.

Pressures resulting from unrestrained population growth put demands on the natural world that can overwhelm any efforts to achieve a sustainable future. If we are to halt the destruction of our environment, we must accept limits to that growth. A World Bank estimate indicates that world population will not stabilize at less than 12.4 billion, while the United Nations concludes that the eventual total could reach 14 billion, a near tripling of today's 5.4 billion. But, even at this moment, one person in five lives in absolute poverty without enough to eat, and one in ten suffers serious malnutrition.

No more than one or a few decades remain before the chance to avert the threats we now confront will be lost and the prospects for humanity immeasurably diminished.

WARNING

We the undersigned, senior members of the world's scientific community, hereby warn all humanity of what lies ahead. A great change in our stewardship of the Earth and the life on it is required, if vast human misery is to be avoided and our global home on this planet is not to be irretrievably mutilated.

WHAT WE MUST DO

Five inextricably linked areas must be addressed simultaneously:

- **We must bring environmentally damaging activities under control to restore and protect the integrity of the Earth's systems we depend on.**
- We must, for example, move away from fossil fuels to more benign, inexhaustible energy sources to cut greenhouse gas emissions and the pollution of our air and water. Priority must be given to the development of energy sources matched to Third World needs -- small-scale and relatively easy to implement.
- We must halt deforestation, injury to and loss of agricultural land, and the loss of terrestrial and marine plant and animal species.
- **We must manage resources crucial to human welfare more effectively.**
- We must give high priority to efficient use of energy, water, and other materials, including expansion of conservation and recycling.
- **We must stabilize population.**
- This will be possible only if all nations recognize that it requires improved social and economic conditions, and the adoption of effective, voluntary family planning.
- **We must reduce and eventually eliminate poverty.**
- **We must ensure sexual equality, and guarantee women control over their own reproductive decisions.**

DEVELOPED NATIONS MUST ACT NOW

The developed nations are the largest polluters in the world today. They must greatly reduce their overconsumption, if we are to reduce pressures on resources and the global environment. The developed nations have the obligation to provide aid and support to developing nations, because only the developed nations have the financial resources and the technical skills for these tasks.

Acting on this recognition is not altruism, but enlightened self-interest: whether industrialized or not, we all have but one lifeboat. No nation can escape from injury when global biological systems are damaged. No nation can escape from conflicts over increasingly scarce resources. In addition, environmental and economic instabilities will cause mass migrations with incalculable consequences for developed and undeveloped nations alike.

Developing nations must realize that environmental damage is one of the gravest threats they face, and that attempts to blunt it will be overwhelmed if their populations go unchecked. The greatest peril is to become trapped in spirals of environmental decline, poverty, and unrest, leading to social, economic, and environmental collapse.

Success in this global endeavor will require a great reduction in violence and war. Resources now devoted to the preparation and conduct of war—amounting to over $1 trillion annually—will be badly needed in the new tasks and should be diverted to the new challenges.

A new ethic is required—a new attitude towards discharging our responsibility for caring for ourselves and for the Earth. We must recognize the Earth's limited capacity to provide for us. We must recognize its fragility. We must no longer allow it to be ravaged. This ethic must motivate a great movement, convincing reluctant leaders and reluctant governments and reluctant peoples themselves to effect the needed changes.

The scientists issuing this warning hope that our message will reach and affect people everywhere. We need the help of many.

- We require the help of the world community of scientists—natural, social, economic, and political.
- We require the help of the world's business and industrial leaders.
- We require the help of the world's religious leaders.
- We require the help of the world's peoples.

We call on all to join us in this task.

"If we don't halt population growth with justice and compassion, it will be done for us by nature, brutally and without pity—and will leave a ravaged world."
—Nobel Laureate Dr. Henry W. Kendall,
co-founder of Union of Concerned Scientists

Al Bartlett's Laws
Relating to Sustainability

Let us be specific and state that both "Carrying Capacity" and "Sustainable" imply "for the period in which we hope humans will inhabit the Earth." This means "for many millennia."

The Laws that follow are offered to define the term "sustainability." They all apply for populations and rates of consumption of goods and resources of the sizes and scales found in the world in 2005, and may not be applicable for small numbers of people or to groups in primitive tribal situations.

First Law: Population growth and/or growth in the rates of consumption of resources cannot be sustained.

A) A population growth rate less than or equal to zero and declining rates of consumption of resources are a necessary, but not a sufficient, condition for a sustainable society.

B) Unsustainability will be the certain result of any program of "development," that does not plan the achievement of zero (or a period of negative) growth of populations and of rates of consumption of resources. This is true even if the program is said to be "sustainable."

C) The research and regulation programs of governmental agencies that are charged with protecting the environment and promoting "sustainability" are, in the long run, irrelevant, unless these programs address vigorously and quantitatively the concept of carrying capacities and unless the programs study in depth the demographic causes and consequences of environmental problems.

D) Societies, or sectors of a society, that depend on population growth or growth in their rates of consumption of resources, are unsustainable.

E) Persons who advocate population growth and/or growth in the rates of consumption of resources are advocating unsustainability.

F) Persons who suggest that sustainability can be achieved without stopping population growth are misleading themselves and others.

G) Persons whose actions directly or indirectly cause increases in population or in the rates of consumption of resources are moving society away from sustainability.

H) The term "Sustainable Growth" is an oxymoron.

I) In terms of population sizes and rates of resource consumption, the only smart growth is no growth.

Second Law: In a society with a growing population and/or growing rates of consumption of resources, the larger the population, and/or the larger the rates of consumption of resources, the more difficult it will be to transform the society to the condition of sustainability.

Third Law: The response time of populations to changes in the human fertility rate is the average length of a human life, or approximately 70 years. This is called "population momentum."

A) A nation can achieve zero population growth if:
* the fertility rate is maintained at the replacement level for 70 years, and
* there is no net migration during the 70 years.
* During the 70 years the population continues to grow, but at declining rates until the growth finally stops.

B) If we want to make changes in the total fertility rates so as to stabilize the population by the mid to late 21st century, we must make the necessary changes now.

C) The time horizon of political leaders is of the order of two to eight years.

D) It will be difficult to convince political leaders to act now to change course, when the full results of the change may not become apparent in the lifetimes of those leaders.

Fourth Law: The size of population that can be sustained (the carrying capacity) and the sustainable average standard of living of the population are inversely related to one another.

A) The higher the standard of living one wishes to sustain, the more urgent it is to stop population growth.

B) Reductions in the rates of consumption of resources and reductions in the rates of production of pollution can shift the carrying capacity in the direction of sustaining a larger population.

Fifth Law: One cannot sustain a world in which some regions have high standards of living while others have low standards of living.

Sixth Law: All countries cannot simultaneously be net importers of carrying capacity. World trade involves the exportation and importation of carrying capacity.

Seventh Law: A society that has to import people to do its daily work ("we can't find locals who will do the work.") is not sustainable.

Eighth Law: Sustainability requires that the size of the population be less than or equal to the carrying capacity of the ecosystem for the desired standard of living.
A) Sustainability requires an equilibrium between human society and dynamic but stable ecosystems.
B) Destruction of ecosystems tends to reduce the carrying capacity and/or the sustainable standard of living.
C) The rate of destruction of ecosystems increases as the rate of growth of the population increases.
D) Affluent countries, through world trade, destroy the ecosystems of less developed countries.
E) Population growth rates less than or equal to zero are necessary, but are not sufficient, conditions for halting the destruction of the environment. This is true locally and globally.

Ninth Law: The lesson of "The Tragedy of the Commons"
The benefits of population growth and of growth in the rates of consumption of resources accrue to a few; the costs of population growth and growth in the rates of consumption of resources are borne by all of society.
A) Individuals who benefit from growth will continue to exert strong pressures supporting and encouraging both population growth and growth in rates of consumption of resources.
B) The individuals who promote growth are motivated by the recognition that growth is good for them. In order to gain public support for their goals, they must convince people that population growth and growth in the rates of consumption of resources, are also good for society. (This is the Charles Wilson argument: if it is good for General Motors, it is good for the United States.)

Tenth Law: Growth in the rate of consumption of a non-renewable resource, such as a fossil fuel, causes a dramatic decrease in the life-expectancy of the resource.
A) In a world of growing rates of consumption of resources, it is seriously misleading to state the life-expectancy of a non-renewable resource "at present rates of consumption," i.e., with no growth. More relevant than the life-expectancy of a resource is the expected date of the peak production of the resource, i.e. the peak of the Hubbert curve.

B) It is intellectually dishonest to advocate growth in the rate of consumption of non-renewable resources while, at the same time, reassuring people about how long the resources will last "at present rates of consumption." (zero growth)

Eleventh Law: The time of expiration of non-renewable resources can be postponed, possibly for a very long time, by:
A) technological improvements in the efficiency with which the resources are recovered and used
B) using the resources in accord with a program of "Sustained Availability,"
C) recycling
D) the use of substitute resources.

Twelfth Law: When large efforts are made to improve the efficiency with which resources are used, the resulting savings are easily and completely wiped out by the added resources that are consumed as a consequence of modest increases in population.
A) When the efficiency of resource use is increased, the consequence often is that the "saved" resources are not put aside for the use of future generations, but instead are used immediately to encourage and support larger populations.
B) Humans have an enormous compulsion to find an immediate use for all available resources.

Thirteenth Law: The benefits of large efforts to preserve the environment are easily canceled by the added demands on the environment that result from small increases in human population.

Fourteenth Law: Second Law of Thermodynamics: When rates of pollution exceed the natural cleansing capacity of the environment, it is easier to pollute than it is to clean up the environment.

Fifteenth Law: Eric Sevareid's Law: The chief cause of problems is solutions.
A) This law should be a central part of higher education, especially in engineering.

Sixteenth Law: Humans will always be dependent on agriculture. (This is the first of Malthus' two postulata.)
A) Supermarkets alone are not sufficient.
B) The central task in sustainable agriculture is to preserve agricultural land.
The agricultural land must be protected from losses due to things such as:
i) Urbanization and development
ii) Erosion
iii) Poisoning by chemicals

Seventeenth Law: If, for whatever reason, humans fail to stop population growth and growth in the rates of consumption of resources, Nature will stop these growths.

A) By contemporary western standards, Nature's method of stopping growth is cruel and inhumane.

B) Glimpses of Nature's method of dealing with populations that have exceeded the carrying capacity of their lands can be seen each night on the television news reports from places where large populations are experiencing starvation and misery.

Eighteenth Law: In local situations within the U.S., creating jobs increases the number of people locally who are out of work.

A) Newly created jobs in a community temporarily lowers the unemployment rate (say from 5% to 4%), but then people move into the community to restore the unemployment rate to its earlier higher value (of 5%), but this is 5% of the larger population, so more individuals are out of work than before.

Nineteenth Law: Starving people don't care about sustainability.

A) If sustainability is to be achieved, the necessary leadership and resources must be supplied by people who are not starving.

Twentieth Law: The addition of the word "sustainable" to our vocabulary, to our reports, programs, and papers, to the names of our academic institutes and research programs, and to our community initiatives, is not sufficient to ensure that our society becomes sustainable.

Twenty-First Law: Extinction is forever.